KU-792-329

# theatre & globalization

BLACKBURN COLLEGE LIBRARY

## REFERENCE COPY

NOT TO BE REMOVED FROM THE LIBRARY

*Theatre &*

Series Editors: Jen Harvie and Dan Rebellato

*Published*

Colette Conroy: *Theatre & the Body*
Jill Dolan: *Theatre & Sexuality*
Helen Freshwater: *Theatre & Audience*
Jen Harvie: *Theatre & The City*
Nadine Holdsworth: *Theatre & Nation*
Erin Hurley: *Theatre & Feeling*
Joe Kelleher: *Theatre & Politics*
Ric Knowles: *Theatre & Interculturalism*
Helen Nicholson: *Theatre & Education*
Lionel Pilkington: *Theatre & Ireland*
Paul Rae: *Theatre & Human Rights*
Dan Rebellato: *Theatre & Globalization*
Nicholas Ridout: *Theatre & Ethics*

*Forthcoming*

Susan Bennet: *Theatre & Museums*
Dominic Johnson: *Theatre & the Visual*
Caoime McAvinchey: *Theatre & Prison*
Bruce McConachie: *Theatre & Mind*
Juliet Rufford: *Theatre & Architecture*
Rebecca Schneider: *Theatre & History*

---

**Theatre& Series**
Series Standing Order
**ISBN 978–0–230–20327–3**

You can receive future titles in this series as they are published
by placing a standing order. Please contact your bookseller or,
in case of difficulty, write to us at the address below with your
name and address, the title of the series and the ISBN quoted
above.                •

Customer Services Department, Macmillan Distribution Ltd
Houndmills, Basingstoke, Hampshire RG21 6XS, England

---

# theatre & globalization

## Dan Rebellato

palgrave
macmillan

© Dan Rebellato 2009
Foreword © Mark Ravenhill 2009

All rights reserved. No reproduction, copy or transmission of this publication may be made without written permission.

No portion of this publication may be reproduced, copied or transmitted save with written permission or in accordance with the provisions of the Copyright, Designs and Patents Act 1988, or under the terms of any licence permitting limited copying issued by the Copyright Licensing Agency, Saffron House, 6-10 Kirby Street, London EC1N 8TS.

Any person who does any unauthorized act in relation to this publication may be liable to criminal prosecution and civil claims for damages.

The author has asserted his right to be identified as the author of this work in accordance with the Copyright, Designs and Patents Act 1988.

First published 2009 by
PALGRAVE MACMILLAN

Palgrave Macmillan in the UK is an imprint of Macmillan Publishers Limited, registered in England, company number 785998, of Houndmills, Basingstoke, Hampshire RG21 6XS.

Palgrave Macmillan in the US is a division of St Martin's Press LLC, 175 Fifth Avenue, New York, NY 10010.

Palgrave Macmillan is the global academic imprint of the above companies and has companies and representatives throughout the world.

Palgrave® and Macmillan® are registered trademarks in the United States, the United Kingdom, Europe and other countries.

ISBN-13: 978–0–230–21830–7 paperback
ISBN-10: 0–230–21830–X paperback

This book is printed on paper suitable for recycling and made from fully managed and sustained forest sources. Logging, pulping and manufacturing processes are expected to conform to the environmental regulations of the country of origin.

A catalogue record for this book is available from the British Library.

A catalog record for this book is available from the Library of Congress.

10   9   8   7   6   5   4   3
18   17   16   15   14   13

Printed and bound in China

**BLACKBURN COLLEGE LIBRARY**

| BB 60559 | |
|---|---|
| **Askews & Holts** | 06-Nov-2014 |
| UCL792.013 REB | |
| | |

# contents

# series editors' preface

The theatre is everywhere, from entertainment districts to the fringes, from the rituals of government to the ceremony of the courtroom, from the spectacle of the sporting arena to the theatres of war. Across these many forms stretches a theatrical continuum through which cultures both assert and question themselves.

Theatre has been around for thousands of years, and the ways we study it have changed decisively. It's no longer enough to limit our attention to the canon of Western dramatic literature. Theatre has taken its place within a broad spectrum of performance, connecting it with the wider forces of ritual and revolt that thread through so many spheres of human culture. In turn, this has helped make connections across disciplines; over the past fifty years, theatre and performance have been deployed as key metaphors and practices with which to rethink gender, economics, war, language, the fine arts, culture and one's sense of self.

*Theatre &* is a long series of short books which hopes to capture the restless interdisciplinary energy of theatre and performance. Each book explores connections between theatre and some aspect of the wider world, asking how the theatre might illuminate the world and how the world might illuminate the theatre. Each book is written by a leading theatre scholar and represents the cutting edge of critical thinking in the discipline.

We have been mindful, however, that the philosophical and theoretical complexity of much contemporary academic writing can act as a barrier to a wider readership. A key aim for these books is that they should all be readable in one sitting by anyone with a curiosity about the subject. The books are challenging, pugnacious, visionary sometimes and, above all, clear. We hope you enjoy them.

*Jen Harvie and Dan Rebellato*

# foreword

There's a funny thing happens when you make a piece of theatre. In fact, it's something of a paradox. As a theatre-maker, you try to make every gesture, every word and every move as specific and as concrete as you can. But at the same time you hope that somehow that same gesture/ word/move will have a resonance, something which is completely outside of the specific and the concrete.

Quite where that resonance lies no one seems to be able to agree. For many people who make theatre there is something called 'truth'. They know it when they spot it, even if they can't define it. 'Oh yes, keep that bit in,' they say. 'It feels very true.'

When I first started working in theatre at the end of the 1980s, I was horrified. I was a student of both the well-established school of Marxist aesthetics and the emerging school of postmodernism, both of which saw truths as at best temporary, and at worst as deceptions. And so I cringed to hear my fellow theatre workers using the word 'true' so read-ily. But I got used to it. I guess 'true' was their way of say-ing something was both precise (in the way that a carpenter might use the word 'true') and had a wider significance (in the way that a religion might declare something a truth).

Alongside the word 'true', some people still used the word 'universal'. 'Yes,' they would say, 'this is a very good play about a black British family in South London, but it is also a universal story.' Or another popular word was 'timeless'. 'Yes, it's set amongst the Jewish community of 1940s New York, but it's a timeless story.' But my read-ings in cultural politics and gender studies of the 1980s and 1990s meant that I—and many other people—were sus-picious of the words 'universal' and 'timeless'. 'Universal' was too often used a shorthand for imperial domination. 'We're simply bringing universal values of civilization to backward countries' was a nineteenth-century justifica-tion for European domination of the globe. (And it is still in use today when our politicians justify war.) 'Timeless', too, has often been used to justify the positions of those in authority. What better way to obscure the constantly shift-ing nature of power relationships, to make it seem that your power is unassailable, than to promote the idea of time-lessness? Of course, the people saying that a black British drama or a Jewish American drama was universal or time-less thought they were elevating the work, offering it liberal inclusion. But many of us were suspicious that these words 'universal' and 'timeless' might be agents of oppression, not liberation.

So there we were, in the 1990s, a new generation making theatre. But we'd stopped believing in—or were deeply suspicious of—the words 'true', 'universal' and 'timeless', words that had been the mainstay of British theatre practice for a couple of hundred years.

Maybe—some theatre-makers reasoned—we should try to ignore the resonance bit of the theatre paradox altogether and just focus on the concrete. 'I just want to tell stories about me and my girlfriend,' declared one young British playwright in the 1990s. He wasn't alone in attempting to turn his back on wider resonances. In the world of performance art and its sister disciplines, there were parallel attempts to create solely concrete acts, moments of confession or performative self-harm that presented themselves as private acts: acts that expressed an entirely personal language but in public spaces.

The theatre itself, of course, carried on being a metaphorical medium, even if many of the theatre-makers denied it. For those of us wanting to explore the full concrete/resonant paradox of theatre there seemed to be little available vocabulary: Marxism and postmodernism had sent so many words to the naughty step. When I first started writing plays in the middle of the 1990s narrative itself seemed to be the only really trustworthy concept. 'Story' offered a concrete set of skills to learn but also allowed you to place your work in a wider context, the narrative tradition. Alongside many others, I took thoughts about narrative from sources as diverse as the Jungian Bruno Bettelheim, the playwright David Mamet, the screenwriting teacher Robert McKee and the philosopher Jean-François Lyotard and started writing plays for British stages.

But then something surprising happened. My plays started to be translated widely. They were produced in different cultures and in fresh contexts. I wasn't alone in this. The United Kingdom produced a fresh new batch of playwrights in the 1990s. Although we didn't know it straightaway, this was perfect timing for a new group of theatre writers to emerge as an international force. Many countries, particularly the former communist states, were opening up not only their economies but also their cultural life to the outside world for the first time in decades. As one Russian director said to me, 'We know about British drama up to Shaw, then everything is a blank, and then things start again with Sarah Kane and you.'

Of course, British playwrights were translated and produced internationally throughout the twentieth century. But by the end of the millennium things had reached a dizzying speed. It was a strange feeling for our generation of playwrights. I'd be sitting down to write in my council flat in Camden and as my fingers hit the keyboards I'd suddenly realize that these words would soon be translated into various languages, that my play would be enacted by actors belonging to totally different theatre cultures, watched by audiences of whose concerns and interests I had little understanding. I remember Sarah Kane returning from a stay in New York in 1997. She had finished her play *Cleansed* the day before. Already dramaturges from across the world were on the phone clamouring to read and translate the play.

Gradually, at the end of the 1990s, I saw that I was being presented with the dominant force shaping much of our lives: globalization. In fact, I realized guiltily, I might even be an agent of that same globalization. The Royal Court Theatre in London—home of so much of the new British drama—has been called, because of the number of subsequent productions its writers receive, the Starbucks of playwriting. And sometimes, as I was invited to see my plays produced abroad and then to speak about theatre or to teach playwriting, I felt like I was just another manager of a global franchise. For a while I even found this a block to my writing.

But I've come to realize that travel and translation have been, on the whole, a good thing for my work. The exchange of ideas with theatre workers and audiences around the world and the exposure to varying theatre practices will, I believe, make me a better writer. And I hope that by learning from the outside world and in doing so producing better work, my plays will challenge theatre-makers in other countries to make better work themselves. Through international exchange, a sort of virtuous circle can happen.

I've found something to replace true, universal and timeless as the other part of the theatre paradox. Resonance for me now lies in the international. I am fascinated by the way a work mutates and is reborn through translation and re-production. I think, now, when I make a piece of theatre there is always the concrete; that is the beginning: how this particular actor with this particular audience can use this word or this gesture to better capture the sense of being alive at this moment in this city in this culture. But there is also the resonant. And this resonant is for me: I wonder what this will mean in other countries and cultures?

I am opposed to many forms of globalization. But I am a committed advocate of—and Dan Rebellato's book has crystallized this beautifully for me—cosmopolitanism. I heartily recommend this book. Its arguments are clear, committed and engaging. And there are some very good jokes. You're in for a treat.

*Mark Ravenhill is a playwright of international reputation whose works include Shopping and Fucking, Some Explicit Polaroids, The Cut, Product, Citizenship, pool (no water), Shoot/Get Treasure/Repeat, and Over There.*

# theatre & globalization

## Artaud at the Balinese theatre

In early August 1931, on the outskirts of Paris, the actor, writer, and would-be director Antonin Artaud went to the theatre.

In 1931 the European empires were at their peak. Between them, Britain, France, Germany, Spain, Portugal, Belgium, the Netherlands, and Italy ruled over most of the world. Although these empires had been acquired through the brutal occupation of other lands and the enslavement of their people, the empire-builders preferred to present their activities as fundamentally civilizing. Since the mid-nineteenth century, one of the most successful ways of doing this had been to mount large-scale exhibitions bringing together information about these colonized territories. These exhibitions tended to display the 'exoticism' of non-European cultures within a story of Europe-inspired progress.

France organized just such an exhibition in 1931. The Paris International Colonial Exposition was held in a specially prepared site in the Bois de Vincennes to the east of Paris and ran for around six months, to the end of the year. Not all European nations were represented: Britain, Germany, and Spain declined to be involved. Nevertheless, in the eighteen-square-kilometre site there were areas representing the colonial possessions of France, Belgium, Denmark, Italy, Portugal, and the Netherlands. Italian theatre scholar Nicola Savarese's book *Paris/Artaud/Bali* (1997) records how the Exposition took three years to plan and build, and how the Metro was extended to bring visitors, eight million of whom were seduced by the publicity's invitation to 'travel the world in a single day' (p. 54). There were information displays and photographs; there were examples of architecture, costume and artwork; and – one of the biggest draws – there were performances.

In the Dutch East Indian Pavilion, a fifty-one-strong troupe of Balinese dancers, under the leadership of Prince Tjokorda Gde Raka Soekawati, performed a mixture of traditional dances (the *legong* and *calonarang*) as well as some more recent styles (*kebyar* and *janger*), to the accompaniment of a gamelan orchestra. In his meticulous reconstruction of this performance, Savarese notes that although the newspapers tended to dismiss the Exposition's performances as tourist fodder, the Balinese company were an exception in their skill and authenticity. It was here that Antonin Artaud went to the theatre.

Artaud was dissatisfied with the theatre around him. He had a vision of a theatre that was stripped of the cultural noise of Parisian middle-class society, with its conventions, its triviality, its orderliness and safety. He longed for a theatre of the utmost seriousness and directness, with roots in something primal and universal: a theatre that would infect its audience like a plague, unmaking society around it. When he went to see the Balinese theatre, he believed he had found it. In his article on the performance published in October that year, and later revised and collected in his great manifesto *The Theatre and Its Double* (1974), Artaud described the Balinese performance as 'the finest demonstration of pure theatre that we have ever been privileged to see here' (p. 41).

Artaud's encounter with the Balinese theatre at the Colonial Exposition in Paris is one of the most celebrated and controversial encounters in modern European theatre. In recent years, theatre scholars have tended to consider it an instance of theatrical 'interculturalism': the contested and controversial history of Western theatre's attempt to co-opt (usually) Asian theatre forms to reinvigorate its own culture. But since then another term has come into use which might also provide a way of thinking through the relationship between the theatre and the world: 'globalization'.

This book is about theatre and globalization. On the face of it, you could be forgiven for wondering whether there is a book to be written on that topic, given the massive disparity of scale between the stubborn localness of the theatre and the awesome scale of the whole world. My approach falls into five sections. First, I compare and choose between various definitions of globalization that are in circulation; second, I trace the history of globalization and several ways in which theatre has responded to it; third, I consider arguments for and against globalization; fourth, I look at two critical and theatrical models for resisting globalization – localization and cosmopolitanism – arguing in favour of the latter; and fifth, I suggest some ways in which theatre and performance might embody this cosmopolitan resistance.

So, first we need to know what globalization is.

## What is globalization?

The word 'globalization' is almost as widespread as the phenomenon it describes. For that reason, the word has accrued a great variety of meanings, and great disagreements surround what it might signify. Some people think it is as old as civilization; some think it is younger than a single generation. Some believe it is the royal road to universal wealth and prosperity; others, that it will destroy us all. As the word suggests, globalization is to do with the 'becoming-worldwide' of things, but which things? There are many answers to this question, but I want to focus on five of them: consciousness, culture, conflict, politics and money.

Some see globalization primarily as an expansion of consciousness. Anthony Giddens describes 'the intensification of worldwide social relations in such a way that local happenings are shaped by events occurring many miles away and vice versa' (p. 64), and for Roland Robertson the term refers to 'the compression of the world and the intensification of consciousness of the world as a whole' (p. 8; see also Steger, p. 13; Waters, p. 5). It is unquestionably true that all parts of the world are more aware of all other parts of the world than they would have been, say, a hundred years ago. For some this awareness is forced upon us by crises, such as global warming, which have catastrophically demonstrated how interconnected we are – but we might also see the growth of our understanding and experience as fostering a gradual widening of our moral attention to and respect for others. This consciousness of others can be hugely enriching – as it seemed to be for Artaud – or it can be the grounds for fear and resentment.

Others see globalization as mainly cultural: the interconnection of world cultures, perhaps even the development of a 'world culture'. This interconnection can be viewed negatively – as the growing homogenization of world cultures (the US sitcom *Friends* is shown in more than half the countries of the world) – or positively in terms of the growing exchange or hybridization of cultures. Artaud's encounter with Balinese theatre might be seen as a positive example of cultural exchange or, negatively, as inevitably coloured by the colonial and imperialist framework of the Exposition.

For some thinkers, globalization centrally involves conflict between ways of life which, in earlier eras, were able to live somewhat separately but, in a world increasingly linked by commerce and communication, come into contradiction with one another in unprecedented ways. This was most famously expressed by Samuel Huntington in his 1993 essay 'The Clash of Civilizations?' and his thesis gained much urgency with acts of global terrorism such as 9/11 and the controversial response of some Western powers in the so-called War on Terror. Artaud saw a productive clash between the purity of the Balinese performance and 'everything that is dirty, brutish and ignominiously chewed up on the European stage' (p. 47). Other ways of expressing the clash between cultures are expressed in the titles of books on globalization such as Benjamin Barber's *Jihad vs McWorld* (1995) and Thomas L. Friedman's *The Lexus and the Olive Tree* (1999).

For others, globalization is a political phenomenon. Over the past hundred years, we have developed several international political institutions: the United Nations, the European Union, and the African Union, among others. They represent to some a decisive step beyond the narrow constraints of national identification and towards a larger sense of membership of the world as a whole. This identification is much contested and is in no sense complete, but for writers such as Jürgen Habermas in *The Postnational Constellation* (2001), giving up 'the nation' as our primary form of geo-political organization is vital for the healthy development of global democracy. The democratic aspect may be fairly new, but types of supra-national government have existed for millennia in the form of empires, perhaps from the Assyrians in 2000 BCE right up to the European empires of the twentieth century, many of which were displayed at the Paris Exposition.

And finally, there is the view that globalization is primarily about money. Wayne Ellwood in his *No-Nonsense Guide to Globalization* (2001) identifies as key elements 'the integration of the global economy ... the dismantling of trade barriers and the expanding political and economic power of multinational corporations' (p. 12). This position says that what is really going on is the development of a global market for goods and services. We live in a world where raw materials may be extracted in one country, shipped to a second to be refined, to a third to be made into goods, to a fourth to be branded, and to a fifth to be sold. Such a reading would want to explore the economic foundations of the Paris Exposition, noting perhaps that the various areas of the park were rather like a kind of international marketplace, each country showing off its wares, attempting to establish its colonial 'brand'. (The French Pavilion included a spectacular reconstruction of the twelfth-century Cambodian temple the Angkor Wat, and it was rumoured that the costs were offset by a film studio that promised to buy the construction so they could burn it down at the climax of a movie. This alliance between money and cultural vandalism may be an example of capitalism's genius for what Joseph Schumpeter called 'creative destruction' [pp. 81–6].)

Of course, these definitions are not mutually exclusive. Evidence suggests that all these changes are happening in the world, so perhaps it is best to see globalization as a collection of different phenomena? Indeed, this is how the term tends to circulate in popular discourse. On the radio in the summer of 2008, within a couple of days, I heard it used to explain the rise of Islamic fundamentalism, Hurricane Katrina, the enormous wages of Premiership footballers, and the existence of Chicken Tikka Masala. I will be arguing against bundling all these different phenomena together, but before I do, I want to consider how theatre might relate to these competing definitions.

## Theatre and globalization

Given that there are so many different views of what globalization is, you won't be surprised to hear that many wildly different connections have been drawn between it and the theatre.

The ever-greater interconnectedness of theatre cultures is visible in the post-war phenomenon of the international festival – such as those in Avignon, Dublin, Edinburgh, Venice, Istanbul, and elsewhere (Harvie, pp. 74–111) – or in international hit plays being performed in different countries in rapid succession – such as Yasmina Reza's *Art* (Comédie des Champs-Élysées, Paris, 1994) or Eve Ensler's *The Vagina Monologues* (HERE Arts Center, New York, 1996). We can see it, too, in the global scale of enormous transnational multi-part performances such as Robert Wilson's *the CIVIL warS*, whose various parts premiered in Rotterdam, Cologne, Rome and Minneapolis between 1983 and 1984, or Societas Raffaello Sanzio's *Tragedia Endogonidia*, whose eleven episodes premiered respectively in Cesena, Avignon, Berlin, Brussels, Bergen, Paris, Rome, Strasbourg, London, Marseille, and Cesena between 2002 and 2004.

The theatre has been a site of global conflict, in controversial productions such as Peter Brook's *The Mahabharata* (Avignon Festival, 1985), the adaptation of a sacred Hindu text, which toured to international acclaim, but also to ferocious accusations of 'orientalism': a distorted and patronizing view of the East that serves ultimately to confirm the West's superiority. In 2002, a theatre literally became a site of conflict when separatist militants from Chechnya, who wanted to break away from Russian control, stormed a Moscow theatre and took the entire audience hostage.

The theatre might be thought to contribute to the globalization of politics through plays that critically represent the workings of globalization, such as Manjula Padmanabhan's satire on the international trade in human organs *Harvest* (Karolous Koun Theatre, Athens, 1999), Drew Pautz's comedy about branding and free markets *Someone Else's Shoes* (Soho Theatre, London, 2007), or Lucy Prebble's portrait of corporate greed *Enron* (Minerva Theatre, Chichester, UK, 2009). On the other hand, some claim globalization is best understood as itself having taken on a theatrical form, with the global system writing the script, directing everyone's entrances and exits, and casting some people in the leading roles and the rest as spear-carriers (Valaskakis, p. 153; Chaudhuri, p. 172).

The theatre has been affected by the globalization of the economy just as everything else has. We see this in the franchising of international 'megamusicals', such as *The Lion King*, which are given near-identical productions in dozens of different theatres across the world. Maurya Wickstrom, in *Performing Consumers* (2006), argues that as consumers we have become quasi-theatrical in the way we 'perform' in the vast themed shopping experiences of advanced global capitalism. Others have claimed that the theatre is best understood as a key part of the 'branding' of world cities, an intangible asset that helps promote business relocations, tourism, and international corporate meetings (Travers, pp. 16–17; Bennett).

Can all these be examples of theatre engaging with globalization? The problem is that there is such diversity in the examples that to embrace them all leaves us with a uselessly capacious definition. The discrepancies can be extreme. There are advocates of the view that the most significant thing about the theatre is that it is *not* global, but firmly, resistantly *local*, but there are also those who point out that performance of one kind or another has been found in all cultures across the world and stretches back more than 20,000 years with the emergence of codified ritual practices: perhaps the theatre is the most globalized expression of human culture there is. It is clear we need to make some decisions about what globalization is.

### It's the economy, stupid

My argument in this book is that not all the developments that I have described should be included under the heading 'globalization'. I want to argue that globalization is a specifically *economic* phenomenon. This is not to say that those other things (culture, politics, consciousness, and so on) are either unconnected or unimportant. Some of them are connected in that they are promoted and furthered by economic globalization (it is not impossible that I could manage to read a Russian novel or eat Thai food without there being a global market, but the global market has made it easier for me to do so). They are also, I believe, extremely important, in fact fundamentally more important than economics. However, I think they are part of a separate force running through human history, which I will refer to as 'cosmopolitanism'. The central argument of this book is that globalization, as an economic phenomenon, is opposed by the counter-tradition of cosmopolitanism and that theatre and performance, for the most part, falls under the latter rather than the former.

I think it is possible to separate globalization and cosmopolitanism in this way for two reasons. First, the chronologies do not tally at all well. In the second century BCE, the Greek historian Polybius noted the significance of the 140th Olympiad, which had begun in 220 BCE: 'In earlier times the world's history had consisted, so to speak, of a series of unrelated episodes, the origins and results of each being as widely separated as their localities, but from this point onwards history becomes an organic whole' (p. 43). Around 1,800 years later, the Italian scientist and philosopher Geminiano Montanari wrote in his treatise *On Money* (1683), 'Intercourse between nations spans the whole globe to such an extent that one may almost say all the world is but a single city in which a permanent fair comprising all commodities is held' (quoted in Marx, *Grundrisse*, p. 782). However dubious their judgements may have been, both these men clearly experienced their world as shrinking, becoming increasingly connected. However, the economic forces of globalization as we know it now do not really go back any further than the late eighteenth century. If globalization and cosmopolitanism were part of the same phenomenon you might expect them to share at least a rough chronology. But the histories are widely divergent.

Second, our attitudes to economic and cultural phenomena are independent of each other. You can coherently disapprove of one and approve of the other. Even if you like or dislike them both, you are unlikely to do so for the same reasons. The reasons to dislike McDonald's are somewhat different from the reasons to dislike drawing world maps. A confusion between the two processes is sometimes exploited by advocates of globalization who like to pretend that if you're against globalization in the form of child labour or sweatshops then you must also somehow be against listening to Brazilian music and eating sushi.

For these reasons, I want to restrict my definition of globalization to the economic. In fact, I'm going to be even more specific: globalization is *the rise of global capitalism operating under neoliberal policy conditions*. Or, in the words of Bill Clinton's presidential campaign strategy, it's the economy, stupid. I explain the implications of this description in a moment, but first I need to introduce the source of the definition, history's most influential philosopher of globalization.

### Karl Marx

Despite living his entire life in the nineteenth century, Karl Marx has turned out to be a compelling theorist of the twenty-first century. And you don't have to take my word for it. An investment banker, quoted in a 1997 *New Yorker* article entitled 'The Return of Karl Marx', declared, 'The longer I spend on Wall Street, the more convinced I am that Marx was right' (quoted in Wheen, p. 5). The World Bank opened their 1996 World Development Report, *From Plan to Market*, with a quotation from *The Communist Manifesto*. In his book *The Crisis of Global Capitalism* (1998), the international speculator George Soros declared that 'Marx and Engels gave a very good analysis of the capitalist system 150 years ago, better in some ways, I must say, than the equilibrium theory of classical economics' (p. xxvi).

If you know anything about Karl Marx, you'll know that he foresaw the joyful overthrow of capitalism, so it may seem strange that an investment banker, the World Bank, and the ninety-seventh-richest man in the world are all lining up to endorse someone who wished only for their downfall. It may seem equally curious that Marx should have been so highly lauded less than a decade after the communist nations set up in his name had collapsed so spectacularly. It may be, as some have argued, that the Soviet Union and the other so-called communist states were established in such an un-Marxist way that their collapse was a vindication of his position, and I think there is some truth in this argument. But, more crucially, Marx's reputation as a political and economic theorist grew rapidly during the 1990s because of globalization.

*The Communist Manifesto* of 1848, written by Karl Marx and Friedrich Engels, declares:

> Modern industry has established the world-market. ... The bourgeoisie has through its

exploitation of the world-market given a cosmopolitan character to production and consumption in every country. To the great chagrin of the
Reactionists, it has drawn from under the feet of
industry the national ground on which it stood.
All old-established industries have been destroyed
or are daily being destroyed. They are dislodged
by new industries, whose introduction becomes a
life-and-death question for all civilized nations, by
industries that no longer work up indigenous raw
material, but raw material drawn from the remot-
est zones; industries whose products are consumed,
not only at home, but in every quarter of the globe.
In place of the old wants, satisfied by the productions of the country, we find new wants, requiring
for their satisfaction the products of distant lands
and climes. In place of the old local and national
seclusion and self-sufficiency, we have intercourse
in every direction, universal interdependence of
nations. And as in material, so in intellectual production. The intellectual creations of individual
nations become common property. National one-
sidedness and narrow-mindedness becomes more
and more impossible, and from the numerous
national and local literatures, there arises a world
literature (Marx, *Selected Writings*, pp. 248–9)

I have quoted this famous passage at length to give a sense of
just how remarkable Marx and Engels's predictions were. In

sentence after sentence, they enumerate forces which were only beginning to be felt in their own time but have run rampant in ours: local industries uprooted by the power of global capitalism; the global nature of production, distribution, and exchange; the continual transformation of our needs and wants; the growing interdependence of the world; the development of international culture as we find ourselves more and more easily able to read novels, see films, and watch theatre from the other side of the world. National boundaries, they seem to be saying, are becoming meaningless; the world is becoming one.

Those who know Marx as a critic of capitalism might be surprised at how positive he sounds about all this. This tone is maintained throughout the first section of *The Communist Manifesto*, because Marx's claim is that the extraordinary productive forces harnessed and exploited by capitalism are driving us towards a truer and fuller appreciation of ourselves.

> All fixed, fast-frozen relations, with their train
> of ancient and venerable prejudices and opinions,
> are swept away, all new-formed ones become
> antiquated before they can ossify. All that is solid
> melts into air, all that is holy is profaned, and man
> is at last compelled to face with sober senses, his
> real conditions of life, and his relations with his
> kind. (p. 248)

What capitalism does by trampling the old traditional social forms is create the conditions under which old superstitions and false understandings of the world can be discarded and new ideas put in their place; vitally, it also brings into being the material conditions whereby these new ideas can be acted on and made real. Most crucially, says Marx, one of the last myths is that capitalism is the only way of running a society. The understanding unleashed by capitalism will ultimately destroy capitalism: 'what the bourgeoisie, therefore, produces, above all, is its own grave-diggers' (p. 255).

What drives capitalism on? For Marx, the terrible genius of capitalism lies in its basic structure. Capitalism may be defined as a system of industrial production where one class – the bourgeoisie – own the 'means of production' (that is, the buildings, the tools, the machinery, the raw materials) and the other class – the proletariat – own only their labour. This gives the bourgeoisie the upper hand, which they use to pay the proletariat as little as they can get away with. Why? Because capitalism thrives on competition: if one manufacturer pays more to its workers, it must either pass those additional costs on to the customer (who will then turn to its rivals' products) or let those costs cut into its profits (which leaves the manufacturer less money to spend on developing new products and new technology, rendering it uncompetitive against its rivals). In other words, capitalism has an inbuilt dynamic that drives down the costs of production and creates huge incentives to innovate. This is the engine that has driven capitalism into every corner of our lives and every corner of the globe, seeking new ways of making new things, more and more cheaply, to gain more and more profit. It is the engine that has turned capitalism into global capitalism and is thus the mechanism driving globalization.

For Marx, then, globalization is nothing new. It is simply capitalism, but where it started by creating markets within particular nations, it has now extended its reach across the world. In nineteenth-century England, there was a divide between the manufacturing North and the administrative South. The North was relatively poor, life expectancy was lower, work was longer, more arduous, and less varied, and access to leisure was more constrained. This divide has been globalized; its remnants cling to the landscape, but most industrial jobs have been exported, and the real north–south divide is now between the global north and the global south. Manufacturing industry and industrial agriculture have moved to regions such as Africa, South America, and South-East Asia. As capitalism moves into its global phase, it wreaks enormous changes upon the world – shattering national boundaries, displacing populations, generating unthinkable new levels of wealth and hardship, revolutionizing the world around us, as Marx said – but it is vital to recognize, too, that there is a deep level of continuity between capitalism and global capitalism: what is true of capitalism will usually be true of globalization. For that reason, I use the terms somewhat interchangeably, since the important criticisms that have been made of capitalism can also, I believe, be made of globalization, only on a much larger scale.

Marx remains the most famous critic of capitalism and the most enthusiastic prophet of its demise. I assess the reasons some have wished to see the end of capitalism a little later, but first I want to explain something of how capitalism developed its global character. This was not a seamless or unbroken development, but encouragingly for our purposes as capitalism slowly revealed its historical character, the theatre was always there to subject it to fierce scrutiny.

## Nineteenth-century globalization

In the early years of capitalism, international trade operated under a loose system of economic controls known as 'mercantilism'. This fell out of favour in the late eighteenth century, in part because of Adam Smith's enormously (and continuingly) influential book *The Wealth of Nations* (1776), which argued that abolishing restrictions to trade would produce not chaos, as had been imagined, but a rational and self-regulating market that would drive down prices, drive up profits, and deliver what people actually wanted.

During the nineteenth century, a lot of the old mercantilist and 'protectionist' laws – such as the Corn Laws that protected British producers against international competition – were abolished in the new *laissez-faire* climate. By the end of the nineteenth century, as industrialization swept across Europe and America, the search for raw materials, cheap colonial labour, and new markets for goods had created a network of international trade routes that linked all the continents of the world.

The theatre reflected this new era of unleashed capitalist profit-hunting. One of the first and most famous plays to represent the new middle class was George Lillo's *The London Merchant* (Theatre Royal Drury Lane, 1731), a play that sits fascinatingly on a faultline between the tragic conventions of the sixteenth century and the melodramatic and naturalistic developments of the nineteenth. The London Merchant of the title is a thoroughly good man, happily named George Thorowgood, with two apprentices: a good and true man, conveniently named Trueman, and the villainous George Barnwell, whose story this really is. The play begins in the business environment but soon takes leave of trade and descends into vice and criminality, because it is Barnwell's lechery, rather than avarice, that leads him to theft and eventually the murder of his uncle. What is clear is that Barnwell and his mistress, whose Lady Macbeth-like urgings compel Barnwell to the gallows, are set up as exemplars of extreme wickedness only to assert the saintliness of the London merchant and the propriety of the honest tradesman.

As capitalism became let loose from its mercantile fetters, the theatre began to ask questions about the morality of money. Edward Bulwer-Lytton's comedy *Money* (Theatre Royal Haymarket, 1840) satirizes the changes in attitude of all those about him when a formerly penniless man, Alfred Evelyn, suddenly becomes extremely wealthy and then appears to lose it all again. Observing how his associates become his great friends when they think he's rich and more distant acquaintances when they believe him to be poor, Evelyn wonders aloud whether money is not coming to replace all other values: 'The Vices and the Virtues are written in a language the World cannot construe; it reads them in a vile translation, and the translators are FAILURE and SUCCESS' (p. 112).

These concerns had flourished into deep pessimism by the end of a century dominated by capital expansion. One principle theme of theatrical naturalism is the power of money to tear apart the moral fibres of ordinary people. This is given cruelly vivid expression in Henry Becque's *Crows* (Comédie Française, Paris, 1882), where a bereaved family are treated as economic carrion by their predatory acquaintances. But money is also a corrosive force in Ibsen's *Pillars of the Community* (Royal Theatre, Copenhagen, 1877), *A Doll's House* (Royal Theatre, 1879), *Ghosts* (Aurora Turner Hall, Chicago, 1882), *An Enemy of the People* (Christiana Theatre, 1883), *The Wild Duck* (National Theatre, Bergen, 1885), and *John Gabriel Borkman* (Suomalainen Teaatteri and Svenska Teatern, Helsinki, 1897). Throughout these plays money causes people to compromise their principles, breaks relationships apart, distorts the truth, and sets a price on human life. (Note, though, that it's a good example of how globalization had taken hold that it took around 125 years for Shakespeare's plays to be translated and performed abroad, but within 10 years of *A Doll's House*'s Danish premiere there had been new productions in, among other countries, Sweden, Norway, Finland, Germany, Austria, Russia, Poland, the United States, the United Kingdom, Belgium, and the Netherlands; see Törnqvist, pp. 173–4.)

Ibsen's *John Gabriel Borkman*, a man who believes that his vision as a financier places him above all morality, had several theatrical heirs, including Mr Voysey of Granville

Barker's *The Voysey Inheritance* (Court Theatre, London, 1905), who sees his embezzlement of company funds to supplement the family income as a kind of investment in the Voysey brand: 'In this world,' he tells his son, 'you must either be the master of money or its servant' (p. 44). In the same theatre and the same year, the millionaire arms manufacturer Andrew Undershaft, from George Bernard Shaw's *Major Barbara*, scorns his priggish son, who is flirting with a career in politics:

> *I* am the government of your country ...: you will do what pays us. You will make war when it suits us, and keep peace when it doesn't. You will find out that trade requires certain measures when we have decided on those measures. When I want anything to keep my dividends up, you will discover that my want is a national need. (p. 124)

By the early twentieth century, the master of money had come to believe he was the master of everything.

And not everyone benefited from the new globalization. In *The Weavers* (Freie Bühne, Berlin, 1893), playwright Gerhart Hauptmann showed a group of Silesian industrial workers whose increasing impoverishment at the hands of global market competition brings them to revolutionary conflict with their industrial masters. And if Hauptmann's weavers were victims of international trade, so too, though in a rather different way, were the declining aristocracy. Their fortunes had been dwindling since the end of feudalism and the disappearance of serfdom; now their only income, from farming and harvesting their land, was suffering as a result of competition with cheaper imports from North America and elsewhere. By the end of the nineteenth century, their expensive stately homes and enormous acreages were burdens. Lady Bracknell, in Oscar Wilde's *The Importance of Being Earnest* (St James's Theatre, 1895), lamented at the end of the century, 'Land has ceased to be either a profit or a pleasure. It gives one position, and prevents one from keeping it up. That's all that can be said about land' (p. 233). In Russia, industrialization's need for a mobile labour force, coupled with the Enlightenment ideas spreading from Western Europe, led to the emancipation of the serfs in 1861, and by the beginning of the twentieth century, Russia's stages were peopled with its insolvent aristocracy: Chekhov's idle, spoiled, and futureless *Three Sisters* (Moscow Art Theatre, 1901); the financially hopeless Ranevskaya, whose servant, Lopakhin, is the only one with the entrepreneurial instincts for making money out of *The Cherry Orchard* (Moscow Art Theatre, 1904); and the pusillanimous Gaevs in Gorky's *Summerfolk* (Passage Theatre, St Petersburg, 1904), idling away their time, oblivious to the poverty and suffering around them.

This battle between nobility and industry is fought out in John Galsworthy's *The Skin Game* (St Martin's Theatre, London, 1920). The protagonist is Hillcrist, a country gentleman from an old family who sets great store by his old-world values: a gentleman, he believes, is 'a man who keeps his form and doesn't let life scupper him out of his standards' (p. 165). But his *sangfroid* is challenged by Hornblower, summed up in the dramatis personae as 'a man newly rich', who threatens to buy up Hillcrist's estate and build an industrial plant on it. When Hillcrist's daughter remarks how fond she is of the house, he retorts:

> Well, you won't be able to live in it unless we stop that ruffian. Chimneys and smoke, the trees cut down, piles of pots. Every kind of abomination. There! (*He points.*) Imagine! (*He points through the French window, as if he could see those chimneys rising and marring the beauty of the fields*) (p. 180)

In a famous auction scene – a tremendous example of capitalism-as-theatre – Hornblower, by mild subterfuge, wrests the land away from Hillcrist. In retaliation the country gentleman uses private information to ruin the Hornblower family, leading to the near-drowning of their daughter. It seems that the aristocracy are not immune from the corrosive effect of capital on personal morality.

## Twentieth-century globalization

The nineteenth century's tentative and piecemeal moves towards a global free market were brought to a halt in the early part of the twentieth century. The three crises of the First World War, the Russian Revolution, and then the Wall Street crash saw capitalism retreat behind national boundaries again. Behind these protectionist barriers, Europe and America rebuilt and prospered into the late 1960s. In the last years of the Second World War, under the influence of the economist John Maynard Keynes, maintenance of this new 'Keynesian' system was handed to the 'Bretton Woods' institutions (named after the venue of the conference at which they were conceived): the International Monetary Fund (IMF) and what is now called the World Bank.

International currency stability was maintained by pegging all currencies to the dollar, and the dollar to the price of gold, which, as a uniformly scarce, durable, and identifiable commodity is pretty stable in value. However, in 1971, facing a massive trade deficit, US president Richard Nixon abandoned this system. This left world currencies to float freely against each other, causing widespread economic and social instability. In 1973, a further blow came with the oil crisis, when the Organization of Arab Petroleum Exporting Countries (OAPEC) announced a policy not to export oil to countries that supported Israel in the Yom Kippur War. The price of oil quadrupled in a year, causing enormous disruption to industrial production across the world.

These shocks had two significant effects on the course of globalization. First, the inability of Western governments to escape their impact brought some aspects of Keynesianism into disrepute and prepared the way for a revival of free-market economic thinking, now known as 'neoliberalism', which would gain a political power base in the government of Margaret Thatcher in the United Kingdom and the presidency of Ronald Reagan in the United States. During the 1980s, both countries saw their economies deregulated, state-owned industries privatized, price and wage controls abandoned, income tax levels reduced, exchange controls dismantled, and many import and export tariffs torn up. These policies spread across Europe and elsewhere during the decade (Harvey, pp. 39–63).

The second effect was a debt crisis. In the more stable climate of the 1960s, several international investors gave out dollar loans to developing countries, particularly in Latin America, for infrastructure development. When dollar inflation bit in the late 1970s, the interest on these loans began to spiral out of control. In 1982 Mexico announced that it was no longer able to make its repayments, and it became clear that many other countries were in the same boat. The possibility arose that widespread default on these international debts might cause a collapse of confidence in the investment banks and the haemorrhaging of the global financial system. At that point, the IMF suddenly re-invented itself as an international debt negotiator. Because the intellectual tide had turned towards neoliberalism, these negotiations took a brutally free-market form. In exchange for offering 'jumbo loans' to these heavily indebted countries, the IMF, with the backing of the US government, insisted that they undertake 'Structural Adjustment Programmes', which meant what the US and UK were doing by choice would be imposed on these countries by economic force: widespread deregulation and privatization, reductions in government spending, and the abandonment of protectionist barriers.

When, at the turn of the 1980s into the 1990s, the Soviet bloc of communist states collapsed, capitalism seemed to be vindicated, and it expanded with unprecedented confidence, to such an extent that some nicknamed its new unfettered expansiveness 'turbo-capitalism'. In a report for the Institute of Policy Studies, Sarah Anderson and John Cavanagh calculated that of the top 100 economies in the world, only 49 of them were countries; the rest were global corporations.

As a result, national barriers have become less and less powerful as a single global market has emerged. In some respects, national identities fade in significance. You can see this in the shopping districts of many world cities: in the omnipresence of certain shops and brands – Nike, Coca-Cola, McDonald's, Nestlé, Nokia, etc. – we see the emergence of a global high street, identical from continent to continent. Sarah Kane's play *Blasted* (Royal Court Theatre Upstairs, 1995) is set in a 'very expensive hotel room – the kind that is so expensive it could be anywhere in the world' (p. 3). This sense of de-territorialized placelessness subliminally prepares us for the great formal shock of the play, that it is set in the same hotel room throughout, but in the first half that room appears to be in Leeds, and in the second half it seems to be, well, somewhere else. This defies ordinary logic in a way that the theatre often does; perhaps, though, there is a kind of globalized dream-work at play here. Just as we struggle sometimes to recount the complexity of our dreams (*you were there ... but you were also my mother ...*), the global high street resembles the geography of our sleeping imaginations (*I was in a street in Mumbai ... but it looked just like Third Avenue ...*).

The British playwright David Hare once argued that the suddenness and force of turbo-capitalism took the theatre by surprise: 'When global capitalism fired up its engines, freed up its markets, kicked up a gear and assumed its historic destiny of infinitely enriching the rich and further impoverishing the poor, then, for a while, culture stood on the kerb, like a vicar whose cassock has been splashed by a passing Maserati' (p. 50). There are relatively few examples of theatre coming to terms with the new world of multinational and global capital. Michel Vinaver's astonishing, kaleidoscopic, eight-hour-long *Overboard* (Théâtre National Populaire Villeurbanne, 1973) mixes business scenes with metatheatrical interludes, dance, and poetic texts to capture the dislocating vast complexity of the new global world. Caryl Churchill's *Fen* (Joint Stock, 1983) explores life in the East Anglian fenland, land which is being sold to international corporations as the play begins. Her *Serious Money* (Royal Court, 1988) is set in the immediate aftermath of the deregulation of the London stock market and tells a complex and ultimately unresolved story of insider dealing, third-world investment, political corruption, and murder. The play is written in loose-limbed, jocular rhyming couplets which capture the crass, cocaine-fuelled, driven energy of the City of London in the 1980s. Plays such as *Serious Money* and movies such as *Wall Street* (dir. Oliver Stone, 1987) are evidence of a rapid turnaround of image for the financial markets. In the 1970s, stockbrokers on British television – think of *Monty Python's Flying Circus*, for example – were invariably dull, suburban, middle-aged, bowler-hatted figures of fun. Within a decade the popular image of the stockbroker was of a young, powerful, aggressive alpha male living on champagne and cocaine and the adrenalin rush of greed: in 1987, Tom Wolfe's novel *The Bonfire of the Vanities* could refer to them — only half-ironically — as the 'masters of the universe'.

Meanwhile, the changing international politics of news-paper ownership were represented in David Hare and Howard Brenton's *Pravda* (National Theatre, 1985) and Doug Lucie's *The Shallow End* (Royal Court, 1997). The ethics of business and sales are subjected to unflattering scrutiny in David Mamet's *Glengarry Glen Ross* (National Theatre, 1983) and Michael Frayn's *Make and Break* (Lyric Hammersmith, 1980). Ping Chong's *Deshima* (Mickery Workshop, Amsterdam, 1990) explores American-Japanese relations across four centuries, ending with a reflexive commentary on the globalization of the art market, which is similarly satirized in Timberlake Wertenbaker's *Three Birds Alighting on a Field* (Royal Court, 1991) and David Williamson's *Up For Grabs* (Sydney Opera House, 2001).

But it is difficult to find more than a handful of plays that *directly* represent globalization, in the way that Granville Barker and Galsworthy's generation had depicted the newly unleashed capitalism. Several politi-cally minded commentators have lamented this lack, David Hare among them, as we have seen. Perhaps this is because globalization is of a different order from the capi-talism depicted by earlier writers. As British playwright Mark Ravenhill writes:

> If you were to take the conflict between capital and labour as a basic motor of human experience ... you

can see how problematic it is to dramatise for a contemporary playwright. Hauptmann could bring his nineteenth-century weavers in conflict with their bourgeois masters by setting his plays in a small German town. ... This is far more difficult today. Where did the food come from that you ate today? Who made your trainers? Who wove that cloth? They are phantoms and the profits have vanished off to phantoms elsewhere. Certainly a very different type of play is needed if we're going to write about this world. (pp. 133–4)

As I shall argue, globalization's effects are so profound that they require – and have generated – wholly different forms to represent them.

Perhaps the most forcible incorporation of globalization's processes into live performance has been effected by performance artists. Often the approach taken has been to mimic or even directly adopt the practices and styles of globalization into the work. The Art Guys are two conceptual performance artists who, in 1998–9, made a work called *SUITS: The Clothes Make the Man* in which they sold advertising space on two business suits which they then wore for a year. Fifty-six companies bought space on The Art Guys at between US$2,000 and $7,000 a slot, including Budweiser, Motorola, and Krispy Kreme doughnuts (http://theartguys. com/SUITS.html). The performance company Gob Squad's installation *I Can ...* (Sean Kelly Gallery, New York, 1998) took the form of a series of video screens on which members of the company offered a number of services – 'I can walk your dog', 'I can tell you a funny story', 'I can fall in love with you', etc. The visual composition resembled a TV shopping channel, and a phone in the gallery connected to a real-time operator who would take your order (you really did have to pay) and arrange for the performance to be carried out (Hoffman and Jonas, p. 66). German theatre collective Rimini Protokoll investigated the connections between global communication and global capitalism in *Call Cutta in a Box* (Zurich Schauspielhaus, 2008), in which 'theatregoers' were led to an office where they held a fifty-minute telephone conversation with a call centre operator in Calcutta.

The stance of these artists is, perhaps deliberately, ambiguous. By foregrounding and aestheticizing these global processes, they seem to be rendering them critically visible and interrogating them, but they may also simply be reproducing globalization's power, yielding to the awesome might of global capital. The performances exist on the edge between resistance and acceptance of the new global world.

## Globalization: for and against

Already I have given you a sense of the ways that the theatre has sometimes criticized capitalism in its national and global forms. In this section, I want to look at the arguments for and against capitalism. I contend that capitalism's flaws mean that we cannot simply accept the system as it is, but it is also important that we acknowledge its many strengths.

First of all, as Marx said repeatedly, capitalism is far and away the best economic system humanity has yet devised, morally far superior to slavery, culturally richer than feudalism, capable of unleashing the human genius for invention and creativity in a way no other system has managed. It is certainly superior to the murderous logic of Soviet so-called communism.

Second, global capitalism's internal drive to innovate and rationalize is an enormous spur to technological innovation, and, by and large, technological innovation is a good thing. In my own lifetime, I have seen the emergence of the home computer, the Internet and email, the mobile phone, soft contact lenses, and the iPod, none of which I would like to do without, and all of which were helped into existence by capitalism.

Third, global capitalism gives us choice. Markets thrive on it. If one company has a monopoly, it has no need to innovate; it becomes complacent and lazy. Competition forces companies to keep innovating, driving down prices and driving up the quality of what they provide. Think how annoying Microsoft software can be, and then think how much *more* annoying it would be if it didn't have Apple nipping at its heels.

Fourth, capitalism has a tendency to generate efficiencies. This is a controversial claim, but it makes sense that if you are trying to cut costs to be as competitive as possible, you will be alert to any kind of waste, generating new processes and systems that do things as simply and quickly as possible. Although it can create enormous hardship at the time, one might feel that the mechanization of certain repetitive tasks is, in the long term, a blessing, since it can take human beings out of some pretty awful, boring, and arduous jobs.

And finally, capitalism is, in a sense, extraordinarily democratic. How often do you get a chance to vote for who governs you? If you live in Britain or America, you probably get to vote for your government or president once every four or five years. Under a market economy, you are expressing your preferences *every single time you make a purchase*. Every second of every day, global capitalism is conducting world-wide referendums on the value of its products, and all we have to do, as consumers, is buy what we want.

However, not all these aspects of capitalism are wholly to its credit or wholly good. First, although it is surely true to say that capitalism is the best economic system yet devised, this does not mean that it is the best *possible* system. Second, although capitalism is a system that supports and encourages technological innovation, it is not itself the creative source of the innovation. Capitalism is a collective human invention, quite as much a product of our inventiveness and creativity as *King Lear* or the Taj Mahal. Praising capitalism for technological advancements is like congratulating a chisel for Michelangelo's *David*.

Is choice a great virtue? *Some* choice is good, but too much choice is stressful and unsatisfying. Put simply, most of us are too busy to gather all the information we need on what we are buying. Faced with a choice of, say, ten different types of mustard, we take a wild guess. This means that whenever we have more than two choices, we are more likely to guess wrong than right. Sometimes we have to guess because information we need has been hidden from us. Most food packaging in Britain, for example, now explains the calorific content and sometimes the country of origin, but it tells us little about the $CO_2$ emitted to get the item to us or the wages paid to those who produced it, both pieces of information that you might consider important. More sinister are the campaigns of disinformation waged by large corporations. Big Tobacco's attempts to foster doubts about the carcinogenic properties of cigarettes are well known. Big Oil is currently, and rather effectively, engaged in a systematic attempt to muddy the waters about global warming (see the Union of Concerned Scientists' 'Smoke, Mirrors & Hot Air' for more information).

What about efficiency? Surely no one could object to that. In its place, efficiency is an excellent thing, but efficiency isn't always what we look for. If I ask a friend who has been having money troubles how she's coping financially, I will be pleased to hear the answer 'I think I'm handling things efficiently'. If I ask a friend who has been having relationship troubles how he's coping emotionally, the answer 'I think I'm handling things efficiently' will strike me as the words of a monster. In many areas of life, efficiency can be an inappropriate goal. Not many people long to go to an efficient party, read an efficient poem, or enjoy a night of efficient passion. What's more, corporate efficiency often means sacking huge numbers of people and exporting their jobs to low-pay regions where workers are treated in ways most of us would consider degrading and subhuman. In many – perhaps most – circumstances, efficiency ranks rather low in our list of requirements.

The claim of capitalism to be democratic is less impressive when you realize that its system is not 'one person, one vote' but 'one dollar, one vote'. It is rather important to Western democracy that Bill Gates gets no more votes than an unemployed single mother and to run politics on the model of the market would be to step backwards 300 years. And in fact, capitalism has no inbuilt tendency to favour democracies, as the number of global corporations that have traded happily with fascists, tyrants, and dictators testifies. Throughout the Second World War, businesses in the US, Switzerland, Sweden, Portugal, Spain, and Turkey continued to do business with Nazi Germany. General Motors' plant in Cologne was turned over to military production, so on D-Day, as Michael Dobbs has shown, US forces in American vehicles were met by Nazi soldiers in the same models. Edwin Black's investigation of IBM revealed that the company supplied the Third Reich with the computing technology that made the Holocaust possible. In the 1990s, British–Dutch oil company Shell colluded with Nigeria's military dictatorship to facilitate its drilling in the Niger delta; armed and financed by Shell, the government conducted a campaign of violence and intimidation against the protestors, most famously the playwright Ken Saro-Wiwa, culminating in his execution, alongside eight others, on trumped-up charges levelled by witnesses that Shell is accused of having bribed with money and promises of jobs (Greenpeace, p. 12).

There are several other systemic problems in the way capitalism works. I will refer to three of them: externality, amorality, and inequality. For the sake of brevity, I outline only the problems, but you can explore these issues further by looking at the suggestions for further reading at the back of this book.

'Externality' is the term economists give to the impact of market transactions on third parties: those 'external' to the transaction. One good example is environmental damage where market exchanges in one country create industrial activity whose impact – say in the form of acid rain – is felt thousands of miles away by people uninvolved in that market. Another externality is unemployment, which tends to be connected to rising rates of crime, homelessness, and social disorder. These costs tend to be carried by national governments, who – rightly – create welfare systems to act as safety nets against market failure, pay for police to combat crime, create social housing, and in various ways foster the kinds of social harmony that business can carelessly damage.

Some advocates of global capitalism claim that a properly functioning free market will generate good, moral behaviour. Eamonn Butler, director of the free-market think-tank the Adam Smith Institute, writes in his short book *The Best Book on the Market* (2008) that 'the market system is a surprisingly *moral* system' (p. 123). In *Good Business: Your World Needs You* (2002), Steve Hilton and Giles Gibbons argue that businesses will act ethically because it is in their interests to do so. If I go to a shop and am short-changed by the shopkeeper, I am unlikely to shop there again and her business will suffer. What this implies is that the shopkeeper will act ethically in order to make a profit. Profit is her primary motive, and the ethics should, all being well, stack up behind it.

But what if all is not well? If the primary motive is profit, in any circumstance where acting unethically is more profitable than acting ethically, the logical thing to do is to lie, cheat, or steal. And this is indeed what many businesses do, as the spectacular scandals in 2002 at Enron, WorldCom, Global Crossing, Tyco, and others showed (and these are only the ones we know about). The credit crunch that triggered a global recession in 2008 was produced by an amazingly small number of US lenders offering mortgages to people who were very unlikely to pay the loan back and then bundling up this 'toxic debt' in complex ways and selling it on. The motive at each point was money, the end-of-year bonus. The longer-term consequences were ignored.

It is even more shocking when the value of human life itself is factored into the calculation of profit and risk. Shortly after midnight on 3 December 1984, following a systems failure at a Union Carbide plant in Bhopal in central India, twenty-seven tons of a deadly gas spilled into the atmosphere. Probably around 8,000 people were dead within a week; 20,000 deaths have been attributed to the disaster since, as well as a host of birth defects, respiratory illnesses, and cancers (Lapierre and Moro). Why did it happen? Several factors have been cited, but poor training of staff, an unmaintained safety system, and the plant's location near a highly populated area were all key contributory factors. Union Carbide was aware of the risks but simply weighed them up against profit.

Despite the claims of apologists such as Butler, Hilton, and Gibbons, global capitalism has no inherent tendency to produce moral behaviour. In 1988, Caryl Churchill's *Serious Money* transferred to the West End of London, and to many people's surprise the theatre was often filled by group parties of City traders who appeared to be having a good time. It has often been suggested that this showed how a politically radical play can be neutralized by the commercial theatre. You could draw a different conclusion, though: that these traders found the play's depiction of them as aggressive, cut-throat, greedy predators straightforwardly accurate and nothing to be ashamed of.

Finally, before I return to discussing the theatre, I want to talk about inequality. Imagine the entire population of the world, all 6.5 billion of us, standing in a line. Rather humiliatingly, we've been asked to stand in order from the poorest person in the world at one end to the richest at the other. Now imagine that the poorest person is asked to put what she owns into a big bucket, then the next poorest person, then the next, until the combined wealth of the poorest half of the population of the world is in that bucket.

Now we skip straight to the rich end of the line. The richest person in the world (currently – November 2008 – Warren Buffet) is asked to put his personal fortune into another bucket, then the next richest, then the next, and so on. How many people do you think it would take before the amount in the second bucket equalled the amount in the first? A million people? A hundred thousand? Ten thousand?

We can estimate the answer by adding up the per capita GDP (Gross Domestic Product) of the world's poorest nations until we get to half the population of the world and then comparing that with *Forbes Magazine*'s annual rich list. Of course, it's an approximation: per capita GDP is an average figure, not all countries are included, different countries report from different years – and, of course, *Forbes*'s list is partly guesswork.

But the answer comes out as 522. To equal the combined wealth of the poorest 3.25 billion people in the world, it would take only the richest 522 people. They could comfortably sit in the Vivian Beaumont Theater in the Lincoln Center, New York, and each could bring a friend. A billion is not a figure most of us are familiar with, so it might make the difference clearer if I tell you that for those 522 billionaires to say their names in turn, one a second, would take just under nine minutes, whereas for the poorer half of the world to say their names would take almost 103 years.

Some point out that poverty at the bottom end has shown signs of slight alleviation, but relative poverty is clearly worse than ever before. The economic historian Angus Maddison in his book *The World Economy* has produced estimates of world GDP that suggesting differences of wealth in the world were fairly small 2,000 years ago and were much the same 1,000 years ago. It was only in the nineteenth century – with the emergence of capitalism across Europe – that the global north pulled dramatically away from the global south, creating the kind of inequalities I've been describing.

The patterns of migration across Western Europe and North America suggest that the global poor are very well aware and unsurprisingly envious of our comfort, nourishment, health, and leisure. It is easy to suggest, as I have been doing throughout this book so far, that in today's world we can all travel to distant places, strike up Internet conversations with friends on other continents, and enjoy food, art, and culture from all the myriad civilizations of the world, but when most people on this planet have never used a telephone, we must recognize that for most people globalization only emphasizes their own poverty and isolation. These types of inequality are destabilizing and unjust, and the situation is not sustainable.

## McTheatre

You might well be thinking that this is all a very long way from the theatre, which, in its quaint artisanal way, pursues a hand-to-mouth existence, on a quite different scale from the operations of transnational finance. In many ways you'd be right. Two key ways that profit is accumulated are economies of scale (making a million tins of beans is cheaper, per tin, than making a thousand) and technological innovation (tins of beans can be produced much more quickly and cheaply by mechanized canning plants than by hand). Economies of scale are very difficult to achieve with the theatre, because performances tend to be unique and hard to reproduce (at least, without turning into TV or cinema). Technology has not helped all that much either: in industrial terms, the theatre is put together in pretty much the same way it was 400 years ago. Technology has not substantially enabled actors to act any faster than they did in Shakespeare's time.

The nearest the theatre has come to being mass-industrialized is in the phenomenon of McTheatre. This is an unflattering term used to refer to the series of global musical theatre hits that include *Cats* (New London Theatre, 1981), *Les Misérables* (Palais des Sports, Paris, 1981), *Starlight Express* (Apollo Victoria Theatre, London, 1984), *The Phantom of the Opera* (Her Majesty's Theatre, London, 1986), *Miss Saigon* (Theatre Royal, Drury Lane, 1989), *Beauty and the Beast* (Palace Theatre, New York, 1994), *The Lion King* (New Amsterdam Theatre, New York, 1997), and *Mamma Mia!* (Prince Edward Theatre, London, 1999). These are sometimes referred to as 'megamusicals'.

The success of these musicals is unquestionable. Each of them has been performed thousands of times in front of millions of people in hundreds of productions in dozens of cities worldwide. *The Phantom of the Opera*, according to its website, has amassed a global box office gross of more than US$5 billion (www.thephantomoftheopera.com), which is about the same as the combined receipts of the current *four* top-grossing movies of all time. McTheatre costs a great deal of money to put on: in 1982, *Cats*'s Broadway production costs were US$5 million, 1994's *Beauty and the Beast* were US$12 million, and *The Lion King* is reputed to have cost US$20 million (Morley and Leon, p. 71; Burston, 'Spectacle', p. 70).

There is something very distinctive and unusual about the way these shows have proliferated around the world. When you buy the rights to put on *Phantom of the Opera*, you're not given a score and a script and told to get on with it; you buy the original production: sets, costumes, direction, lighting, the poster, and all the merchandise. This means that all productions of *The Phantom of the Opera* are, to a very significant extent, identical. This explains the nickname McTheatre, because McDonald's restaurants are opened on very similar terms. These are not new productions; they are franchises.

McTheatre productions are entirely typical of the methods of global capitalism, for good and bad. Let's start with the good. When the producer Cameron Mackintosh began working in British theatre in the 1970s, it was customary, a year or so after a London run had opened, to produce a regional tour; it was also customary that this would be a pale and shabby imitation of metropolitan original. Mackintosh was determined that audiences anywhere in the world should have the same high-quality experience as first audiences did. (This is where the McTheatre/McDonald's parallel is flattering; Mac and Dick Macdonald, when they first started franchising their restaurants, also wanted to gurantee customers a standard of hygiene, taste, and nutrition wherever their burgers were to be found, which is surely a good thing.)

On the other hand, standardization means that many of the usual virtues of theatre are diminished: its liveness, the uniqueness of each performance, its immediacy, its ability to respond to place and time. In place of these virtues, these shows appear almost entirely unchanged wherever they are. Several new theatres have been built specifically to house these shows in cities such as Toronto, Las Vegas, Basle, Denver, Frankfurt, Bochum, Tokyo, Hamburg, and Stuttgart. Building new theatres might seem like a positive contribution to the ecology of world theatre, although the fact they are built for shows that are miked means little attention is paid to their acoustics, making them unusable for most other kinds of theatre. Their enormous seating capacities – 2,000 in the Princess of Wales in Toronto and the Theater im Hafen in Hamburg; an eye-watering 3,000 in the Buell Theatre in Denver – are almost impossible to fill except with a global megahit. In other words, these theatres are purpose-built, and, as many theatre owners have discovered, when that megamusical purpose has gone, all that's left is a large, unfillable white elephant.

The miking of these musicals is also part of their mistrust of space. One of their acoustic characteristics is the level of amplification: they are much louder than earlier musical shows. Indeed, the megamusical invariably amplifies voices and instrumentation to just the volume where miked sound overwhelms the natural acoustics of the space. Most megamusicals are made available in recorded form before their stage debuts – either as a soundtrack album or as a film – and the amplification is designed not to enhance the live experience but to make the live experience a more faithful reproduction of the recording. The result is that the performer is displaced. First, the bombardment of sound through speakers placed all around the auditorium discon-nects the singer from the song. Then the smoothness and consistency of the performer's amplification cover his or her movements on stage and even any sense of the human body from which these sound are issuing (see Burston, 'Theatre Space', pp. 205–18). One of the more extraordinary ver-sions of this came in the global dance spectacular *Riverdance* (Point Theatre, Dublin, 1995), which centred on the com-plex percussive effects of Irish step dancing. The sound of the shoes hitting the floor did not fill some of the larger theatres, and miking at stage level proved ineffective, so pre-recorded taps were played at deafening volume over the dancing, marking a startling new level of alienation of the body from performance.

There is a clear continuity between the methods of pro-duction employed in creating the megamusical and two of the most important innovations in early twentieth-century capitalism: the time-and-motion study and the production line. The time-and-motion study was pioneered from 1899 by Frederick Winslow Taylor, whose method was to observe a worker engaged in a task, break that task down into simple movements, discarding any unnecessary stages, and then retrain everyone to perform the action in the quickest time. 'Bit by bit,' writes one of his commentators, 'the factory worker lost control of his tools, the process of production, even the way he moved his body as he worked' (Gabor, p. 7). The head of the US machinists' union, James O'Connell, argued that this turned the worker into 'a mere machine, to be driven at high speed until he breaks down, and then to

43

be thrown onto the scrap heap' (Kanigel, p. 448). The production line was introduced by Henry Ford in 1913, and it transformed factory production: rather than being involved in a relatively complex series of procedures, each worker was now responsible for a single stage of production, which he would repeat all day. And because all these stages were connected by the conveyor belt, for the first time the tool determined the productivity of the worker, not the other way round. One of Ford's workers, Charles A. Madison, wrote of the production line system as 'a form of hell that turns men into driven robots' (Batchelor, p. 53).

In the McTheatre franchise, the workers have little or no control over their conditions of work; all the creative decisions were taken years ago and are locked down. The choreography is fixed, and the movements are largely determined by the automated sets and standardized lighting designs, which means that any deviation from the pattern risks injury or singing in darkness. Susan Russell, a former megamusical company member, describes it thus: 'I was one of thirty-seven workers who built the standardised product of *The Phantom of the Opera* every night. My function was to replace a missing worker, accomplish their required tasks, and assemble the product without missing a beat, interrupting the flow, or disturbing the rest of the machine' (p. 57). Directors, meanwhile, use little of their training or experience, as they are merely supervising the reconstruction of a show that already exists. It's like asking a chef to supervise the heating up of a ready meal. As one director lamented: 'It no longer is a play any more, it's an *assembly* line! It's a *corporation* ... it's like you're running a branch plant' (Burston, 'Spectacle', p. 75).

The dehumanizing effect of working in McTheatre becomes part of these shows' aesthetic. The human performer is either dwarfed by the set – think of the underground boat trip by candlelight in *Phantom*, the Helicopter in *Miss Saigon* – or masked and disguised as cats, candlesticks, or trains. In a show such as *The Lion King*, the costumes are the stars, and the actors merely their operators. When we think of the megamusicals, we often think of the brand images: the big-eyed orphan, a cat's eyes, a combined Japanese pictograph/helicopter. The star performers are never part of the brand image, because in McTheatre even the biggest star is replaceable.

This turn away from the human is not unique to the megamusical: try watching an evening of commercial television – most advertisements now are designed to be used in a number of different territories, so advertisers devise ingenious ways of not showing people talking, which would limit the advert to one language. Increasingly, we are invited to buy these products by puppets, cartoons, or animals, which are easier to redub. We have also seen the emergence of an international touring theatre in which visual spectacle, physical movement, and music – all of which can appear vaguely meaningful to an international audience – are at a premium: what performance-maker Mike Pearson has referred to as 'air-brushed "Euro-products" that can move anywhere' (Kaye, p. 219).

Two examples illustrate the point. The Blue Man Group were formed in 1987, and their internationally franchised

shows consist of three unspeaking blue-painted performers playing drums, to the accompaniment of loud electronic
music, and throwing a lot of brightly coloured paint around.
The show started, by all accounts, as a kind of performance-
art critique of 1980s culture, but now, with its wordlessness
and its bland corporate rock soundtrack, it seems cynically
designed to communicate frictionlessly to all possible markets. *The Sultan's Elephant* by Royal de Luxe (Nantes, 2005)
was a massive work of puppetry, at the centre of which was
a fifty-ton mechanical elephant, which, when I saw it, plod-
ded around the centre of London, enacting, apparently, some
story about a time-travelling girl and a Sultan of the Indies.
Impressive though the sight was – and delightful in the way it
displaced cars in London for a weekend – it seemed aggres-
sively empty in its half-hearted mixture of Orientalist clichés.

I'm saying little that the makers of megamusicals have
not said themselves. John Scher, the president of Polygram
Diversified Entertainment, unromantically explained his
company's move into theatrical production: 'We are an
entertainment company, and we are looking for product
to feed our systems' (Burston, 'Spectacle', p. 71). Indeed,
increasingly, globalized theatre is not so much an event in
itself as part of a transnational entertainment corporation's
marketing strategy, as becomes clear when we look at the
history of one particular piece of theatre merchandising.

## A short history of the theatre programme

Among the many innovations in the marketing of *Cats* was
the development of the 'cat's eye' brand logo. This image

appeared on posters, T-shirts, the outside of the theatre building, and all associated memorabilia: key-rings, mugs, cast albums, postcards, badges, bags, books, and the souvenir brochure. This last item was a way of avoiding one curious convention in British theatre law: a theatre producer is obliged to provide information for the programme, but all the proceeds from its sale go to the theatre owner. The much more handsome and glossy souvenir brochure was intended to rival the programme, diverting some of the programme sales away from the theatre owner and towards Cameron Mackintosh. The programme also served Mackintosh in another way: placing the *Cats* logo so prominently on the theatre programme ensured that theatregoers carrying the programme home on the Tube or the bus would become walking advertisements for the show. If Andrew Lloyd Webber created the through-sung musical, Cameron Mackintosh must be given credit for creating the through-branded musical.

Eight years later, Cameron Mackintosh opened *Miss Saigon* at the Theatre Royal, Drury Lane. Extremely unimpressed by his own billing in the theatre owner's programme, he decided to rent the shop opposite the theatre and sell all his *Miss Saigon*-branded merchandise there, thus denying the theatre owner any income from the merchandise at all (Morley and Leon, p. 131). This marks a curious shift towards the autonomy of the marketing. Here, the merchandising was, in a sense, competing with the theatre.

Another eight years later and we reach the opening of *The Lion King*. One of the things the megamusical is said to have increased is the time it takes for a show to recoup the producer's initial investment. In 1992, one theatre investor warned that big musicals might take a year before they started making money (Carden and Huntley, p. 18); in 2000, it was suggested that with 80 per cent houses it would take most megamusicals three years to recover costs. But what about *The Lion King*, with its reputed US$20 million production bill and enormously high running costs? How long will that investment take to recoup?

The answer, rather astonishingly, is that it probably never will. The costs of running the show are higher than the average box office. Why would a vast global business like Disney keep such a show going when it's losing money? Because it's not a show; it's an advert. The show does make money, but only by promoting sales of *Lion King* merchandizing: the website links to a shop where you can buy videos and DVDs, baseball caps, books, CDs, fridge magnets, coffee mugs, posters, T-shirts, towels, toys, ornaments, badges, pencil cases, key-rings, pens, and, of course, a souvenir brochure of the show (Burston, 'Spectacle', pp. 71–2). Maurya Wickstrom has written about the unusually strong design continuities between the *Lion King* stage and the Disney Store (pp. 85–9). In only sixteen years, we have seen a complete turnaround. In 1981, *Cats* had a programme which was designed to help sell the show. In 1997, *The Lion King* was a show designed to help sell the programme.

What McTheatre demonstrates is the ruthless inventiveness of global capitalism for transforming everything into a way of making money. This is not wholly to criticize those entrepreneurs; if you can ignore the bland, boring music, *The Lion King* is a visually astonishing piece of theatre. However, we might also think that something is lost when everything is made to turn a profit. Indeed, over the past quarter-century more and more voices have been raised in opposition to globalization.

## The anti-globalization movement

One of the defining features of the era of globalization has been the force and intensity of its opposition. As austerity bit in the 1970s and 1980s, several countries, particular in South America, saw great waves of protests of vary-ing kinds, from demonstrations and marches to general strikes and riots (Walton and Ragin, p. 877). In the 1990s, in the Mexican region of Chiapas, the Zapatista Army of National Liberation, fronted by the mysterious figure of Subcomandante Marcos, was formed to campaign against the North American Free Trade Agreement. In the richer countries, protests began to occur more frequently in the later 1990s, with famous clashes in Seattle in 1999 outside a conference of the World Trade Organization; at the G8 Summit in Genoa in 2001 – the basis for a verbatim play by Italian playwright Fausto Paravidino, *Genoa 01* (Royal Court, 2001); and at an EU summit in Gothenburg, in June 2001, where Tony Blair notoriously described the protes-tors as an 'anarchists' travelling circus'.

It is worth remarking on the very theatrical nature of many anti-globalization protests. Under the loose umbrella concept of 'tactical frivolity' many demonstrations have large numbers of participants dressed in costume: the Black Bloc, you won't be surprised to learn, dress in black; the Tute Bianche wear padded white costumes (not to be confused with the similarly attired Wombles); the Pink Silver bloc bring the glamour of radical queer drag, and anti-globalization activism can also take the form of culture jamming, adbusting, guerrilla gardening, or radical cheerleading. A key figure in the performative resistance to globalization is Reverend Billy of the Church of Non-Shopping, whose flash-mob-like actions against leading global brands have seen him barred from branches of Starbucks the world over (Talen). The Yes Men are activists who dress in sharp city suits and infiltrate gatherings of businesspeople, sometimes managing to get to the podium and deliver speeches that turn the proceedings into farce and expose the participants to ridicule (www.theyesmen.org). The Clandestine Insurgent Rebel Clown Army is a principally British group of activists who blend analysis and ridicule as they lampoon the powerful.

The anti-globalization movement is, however, far from being a coherent entity. Many different viewpoints are represented in this very loose coalition of interests, from anarchists to libertarians, communists to liberals, environmentalists to unionists. Some are on the right, some on the left; many are non-aligned. The coverage of the various campaigns that come under the anti-globalization banner ranges from GM foods to global democratic reform, from third world debt to global warming. The movement is not unified, perhaps because, to borrow the title of Paul Kingsnorth's book about the movement, it is made up of one no, many yeses.

Any attempt to group these positions runs the risk of oversimplification, but I want to draw attention to two distinct and opposing attitudes to how we should respond to globalization. The first is localization; the second is cosmopolitanism. Both have corresponding attitudes to how we should make theatre. I consider localization first.

**Localization**

If the problem is globalization, it seems like a no-brainer that the solution would be localization. If global corporations bestride the earth, destroying local cultures, turning all high streets into copies of each other, degrading the environment, undermining governments' ability to protect their own people, and, worst of all, foisting the work of Andrew Lloyd Webber on us all – I jest, of course – then surely great good will come from reasserting and protecting the local.

What would localization mean in practice? Books such as Colin Hines's *Localization* (2000) and Walden Bello's *Deglobalization* (2004) offer a number of good practical examples of localizing policies. They propose a series of tough trade and exchange controls that would make it extremely expensive to move goods, services, and capital across national boundaries. This would force transnational corporations to work at a local level, making them accountable and therefore responsive to local communities. Both authors favour a revival of local democracy, engaging more people in their local areas so that they are informed enough to express the real demands of their communities. Taxation would be transformed so that it fostered greater equality and wider, more even competition (Bello, ch. 7; Hines, chs 7–12).

One of the key achievements of such a plan would be to tame the environmentally destructive international food industry. Bello cites the figure that the average Western dinner has travelled 2,000 miles before it arrives on our plates (p. 113). The $CO_2$ emissions of the aeroplanes and trucks and cars that transport the food and its customers to the supermarkets are major contributors to global warming. Getting global corporations out of the way will restore governments' ability to act on behalf of their populations, which will do a great deal to resolve the problem of 'democratic deficit', whereby key decisions that affect all our lives are made by institutions that are not democratically accountable to us (for example, as a UK resident, I can vote in local, national, and European elections. I have no such democratic control over General Motors, say, or the governments of the United States or China, though these have a profound effect on my life).

There are reasons to imagine that the theatre is well placed to be a central plank of a localizing cultural policy. 'The politics of theatre is irreducibly local,' writes US theatre scholar William Worthen (p. 167), and indeed theatre's liveness tends to commit it to particular places of performance. This is not an impregnable position, however, and many avant-garde performances test the limits of this liveness (see Philip Auslander's book *Liveness* for a critique of this idea). Moreover, as we have seen, McTheatre inverts the relationship between recorded and live by making the live event a very direct reproduction of a recording. But in broad terms, the uniqueness of each theatrical performance does in some senses tie theatre to place; so, can this be a source of political strength?

I want to talk about two theatre and performance traditions that share aspects of the localization view: community and site-specific performance. I should say that in neither case do their exponents explicitly align themselves with localization as such, but the attitudes expressed overlap sufficiently to make the comparison instructive.

In her important book *Local Acts* (2005), the US theatre scholar Jan Cohen-Cruz defends the particular political value of community theatre, using arguments that are analogous to those offered by advocates of localization. Real community theatre, she says, is in an important sense made *in* the community, *by* the community, and *for* the community: a tough set of criteria that not very much theatre work, not even all community theatre work, would meet. What kind of theatre is she opposing? She evokes the case of a privileged theatre-maker (privileged by virtue of class, education, race, etc.) coming to work with under-privileged communities, using them for research, and then going off to make a piece of theatre elsewhere. Tellingly, she describes the transaction in terms of global corporate exploitation: 'And what do the artists do? – mine the raw material, all that experience and all those stories. Then they leave with the natural resources and make their own art out of them' (p. 91). Instead, she suggests, the theatre-maker should stay within the community, produce the work there, and maybe foster theatre structures that could continue indigenously long after the theatre-maker is gone. Doing so will help promote 'active culture', an active relation to theatre that is perhaps a rehearsal for active citizenship.

On a very different level of cultural activity, the advocates of site-specific performance – that is, performances designed for particular locations such that a relationship with the location is part of the performance – argue that such acts are radically resistant to globalization. The fact that these performances exist only in relation to the space they are in makes site-specific performance a form of theatre that is even harder to commodify than usual. As the artist Dennis Oppenheim said of his site-specific artworks such as *Cancelled Crop* or *Directed Seeding* (1969), both of which took the form of temporary patterns cut or seeded in fields, 'in one gesture it countered major canons of traditional art, such as sellability, accessibility, mobility. I mean, you can't see the art, you can't buy the art, you can't have the art' (Kaye, p. 66).

A particular set of beliefs often accompanies arguments for localization. One is a variety of cultural relativism, which is the view that there are no values in the world that are not relative to a particular culture. What is right in one culture might be wrong in another; what is important in one culture may be trivial elsewhere – hence the danger of imposing uniformity on the world. This breaks down into two related beliefs: one, that the world is indeed diverse in this way (hence localization's emphasis on the local languages, food cultures, customs, and indeed forms of performance that are under threat from globalization); two, that this diversity should be respected and defended.

These arguments are intended to support the regions of the world against cultural imperialism: the physical or mental overwriting of a perfectly healthy culture with inappropriate practices and beliefs drawn from a quite different society. This is something that I – and, I hope, you – would certainly condemn and want to challenge. But do these arguments really stack up? I think not, and I will briefly explain why.

First, localization presumes that our cultures are self-sufficient. But, as Marx says, our needs and wants change as our societies develop, and we have surely developed beyond the point where, say, the English would be happy to subsist on a diet of Lancashire hotpot and Morris dancing. We have come to enjoy the products of the world, and there is nothing inherently wrong with that, I'd suggest. There are important environmental concerns around food miles and air travel, but these are contingent: *if* some emissionless way of transporting these goods were found, then the objection to, say, eating avocadoes out of season would disappear.

Second, by expressing a particular concern for those inside the community, localization entails a certain disregard for those outside it. The BBC television comedy series *The League of Gentleman* is set in a fictional Yorkshire village, Royston Vasey, the edge of which is policed by Edward and Tubbs, the proprietors of A Local Shop for Local People. Confronting all-comers with the interrogation 'Are you local?', they comically represent a local small-mindedness that is the other side of localization. (It also demands strenuous levels of ignorance, as Tubbs discovers when she comes across a map of the United Kingdom and confronts her husband with the terrible

accusation 'You lied to me. There *is* a Swansea!') In some episodes, Edward is prepared to murder to preserve the integrity
of the town. Although I wouldn't accuse localizers of that, if
someone were able to intervene in another culture to prevent
systematic acts of violence but on cultural-relativist grounds
refused to do so, we might equally say they *were* imposing
their moral standards on the people of another culture by not
intervening to protect them.

Third, asserting the values of your own region need not
be politically progressive. It could just as well be brutally
nationalistic. In 1992, a major environmental summit was
held in Rio, and one of its key aims was to establish global limits on fuel consumption. The US was and is the largest fuel consumer in the world, and when, in advance of
the conference, George Bush Snr declared, 'The American
way of life is not up for negotiation' (quoted in Singer,
p. 2), he was asserting the unbending value of the local, to
the great disadvantage of the rest of the world. The truth
is that exploiting regional differences is one way in which
global corporations make money, by producing cheaply in
one region and selling expensively in another, playing on
regional differences to generate short-term competitive
advantage. This would be impossible if there were single
global standards for health and safety, wage minimums, and
corporate governance. Free-market fundamentalists are
themselves often cultural relativists: the neoliberal advocate David Henderson argues against establishing any global
policy standard, calling it 'imposed uniformity' and finding
it particularly malicious 'when it acquires an international

dimension' and when the policies 'extend across borders' (pp. 116, 131). In ethical terms, Henderson speaks just like a localizer.

Finally, and maybe most decisively, this kind of cultural relativism is internally contradictory. Its two beliefs – (1) that all values are culturally relative and (2) that these various cultures should be protected – don't fit together: (2) is an ethical principle and expresses a value, so according to (1) it must be culturally relative, but what culture is it relative to? In fact, it's a *universal* principle. It says that we should respect cultural diversity *everywhere*, regardless of circumstances, irrespective of local conditions! You can't insist that *all* values be devolved down to the local level without contradicting yourself.

This has an effect on how we might see community and site-specific theatre. The artist Richard Serra became embroiled in a famous controversy when it was proposed that his enormous site-specific sculpture *Tilted Arc* (Federal Plaza, New York, 1981) be moved. Serra did not simply claim this should not happen; he claimed it was impossible: '*Tilted Arc* was commissioned and designed for one particular site: Federal Plaza. It is a site-specific work and as such not to be relocated. To remove the work is to destroy the work' (p. 194). I have sympathy for Serra's predicament but, in his anger, I think he overstates his case. After all, if *Tilted Arc* 'is' its relation to that site, what happens when the buildings around the artwork change? Have those architects destroyed his artwork? And how far does the 'site' extend? Fifty metres? Fifty kilometres? More crucially, it may be the case that the artwork is *different* if moved, but *destroyed*?

One might even, using Serra's own arguments, suggest that the dialogue with place must involve a commitment to whatever happens in that relationship and that the removal of *Tilted Arc* is part of the continuing site-specific evolution of that artwork's meaning.

Indeed, many site-specific artworks have proved to work rather well when moved. Fiona Templeton's *YOU – The City* (New York, 1988) is a multilayered performance installation in which one audience member at a time embarks on a two-hour journey through midtown Manhattan, encountering sights and characters that radically defamiliarize his or her experience on those streets. It could hardly be more site-specific, except that the performance has been recreated very successfully on the streets of Rotterdam, Ljubljana, The Hague, Zurich, and Munich. Wrights & Sites are an Exeter-based performance group whose work has sometimes involved creating similarly destabilizing walking tours for people around specific locations, as in *An Exeter Mis-Guide* (2003), a small guidebook that urged the walker to reconceive the city through acts of performance, observation, and imagination. Perhaps spurred by the recognition that these events, although inspired by the city, were not specific to that city, three years later they produced *A Mis-Guide to Anywhere*, introducing an intriguing geographical indeterminacy to the site-specific project. My reflections are not meant to criticize site-specific or community theatre, but to say that theatre and performance are not so readily assimilable to localization as they may first appear.

For all these reasons, localization is an inadequate response to globalization. In political terms it seems to entail our shutting ourselves off from our neighbours in the world. In philosophical terms, it lapses into contradiction. Theatrically, attempts to assert the value of the purely local often involve a hidden – or sometimes more explicit – appeal to something much broader. Some critics have tried to combine the local and the global in the concept of 'glocalization' (see Graham-Jones, p. 8). I am unconvinced. First, combining two bad ideas is not obviously a great way of creating one good one; second, I am not persuaded that you solve genuine global problems by inventing new terminology. It would be like trying to bring about a new world order by inventing a new word order.

Instead, I think the problem is a false opposition between the local and the global. Both are implicated in globalization. The 'other' of globalization is not the local but cosmopolitanism.

## Cosmopolitanism

Diogenes of Sinope was a famously contrary fourth-century BCE philosopher who lived in a tub and professed to think dogs more virtuous than human beings. One of his more enduring pronouncements was made during the negotiations at a slave auction:

> BUYER: First tell me, friend, where do you come from?
> DIOGENES: From everywhere.
> BUYER: What do you mean?
> DIOGENES: That I am a citizen of the world.
> (quoted in Reale, p. 29)

The Greek word Diogenes uses is *kosmopolítēs*, which gives us the modern word 'cosmopolitanism'. Cosmopolitanism is a belief with a remarkably tenacious hold on our imaginations, finding expression in the thought of the Stoics of Ancient Greece and Rome, in all the world's major religions, and in the work of thinkers such as Erasmus, Kant, and, arguably, Marx. It has recently seen a significant revival of interest in the overlapping fields of international relations and globalization.

Cosmopolitanism is a belief that all human beings, regardless of their differences, are members of a single community and all worthy of equal moral regard. Cosmopolitanism also entails a commitment to enriching and deepening that global ethical community. Politically, cosmopolitans tend to argue for a strengthening of international law (on cosmopolitan principles), the development and democratization of institutions to embody that law, say, the International Criminal Court, and nations giving up some of their sovereignty in the name of participating fully in the cosmopolitan community. Cosmopolitans disagree on exactly how these states of affairs can come about: some believe a reformed United Nations might embody this cosmopolitan ideal; others think nothing short of a world state can bring the global ethical community into being.

The most important intellectual influence on modern cosmopolitanism is, perhaps surprisingly, an eighteenth-century German philosopher who is reputed never to have left his home town. Nonetheless, Immanuel Kant's vision of a world united by cosmopolitan principles has left a great impression on current debates. Kant expressed his cosmopolitan ideas in a number of books and essays. In 'Idea for a Universal History with a Cosmopolitan Aim' (1784), he explains how our moral sense develops through history to encompass the whole world. He argues that human beings are ill equipped to survive alone, and that to flourish we are required to work together, though at the same time we jealously guard our autonomy. He calls these contradictory impulses our 'unsociable sociability' (*Anthropology* p. 111 [8:20]). To survive we are forced to produce ever more sophisticated and far-reaching forms of society that can serve both our collective and individual interests. This leads eventually to 'a universal *cosmopolitan condition*, as the womb in which all original predispositions of the human species will be developed' (p. 118 [8:28]). In 'Towards Perpetual Peace', Kant sketched out various principles of international law that would be required for such a cosmopolitan condition to be maintained; these principles are radical and demanding and rest on the fundamental ethical principle that 'a violation of right on *one* place of the earth is felt in *all*' (*Practical*, p. 330 [8:360]).

Some readers will be sceptical of the suggestion that history shows any great trend for human beings to treat one another as objects of moral concern, especially after a century that brought us Russian pogroms, the Great Purge, the Holocaust, Bosnia, Rwanda, and 9/11. These events are indeed appalling and horrifying, but they do not, of themselves, contradict Kant's claim that a fuller sense of our moral commitments emerges from our antagonisms. Some of these events did indeed lead to a new appreciation of cosmopolitan right in such advances as the concept of crimes against humanity, the United Nations, the International Court of Justice, the Convention on the Prevention and Punishment of Genocide, and the Universal Declaration of Human Rights, all of which emerged within three years of the Second World War's end. It is surely right to say that out of these horrors has come a sharper understanding of our moral commitments to one another.

We can see this at work in theatrical terms, too. The oldest surviving play in world theatre is Aeschylus' *The Persians* (City Dionysia, Athens, BCE 472), which dramatizes the attempted invasion of Greece by the Persian king Xerxes and his defeat at the battle of Salamis, less than a decade before the play was written. It is both a local play, focusing on a topical matter of national concern – it would not be unlike seeing a play in 2009 about 9/11 – and an international play, focusing on an encounter between nations. Aeschylus sets his play entirely in the Persian camp in Susa and begins it with a group of elders and their queen waiting fearfully for news of the battle. As the play unfolds, the full scale of the defeat becomes clear to them, and the play culminates in the return of Xerxes, who joins the elders in lamenting their many dead. It is a play of stillness and waiting and slowly releasing grief. Because it features very little dramatic action and there is some ambiguity about whose story we are supposed to be most interested in, some critics have decided that this play is not a tragedy – indeed, they say, rather the reverse: the play is in fact a piece of Greek self-congratulation, what Philip Vellacott, translator of the Penguin edition of the play, calls 'the gratification of the natural pride of the Athenians in their achievement' (p. 17).

If that was the aim of the play, Aeschylus surely failed. The play repeatedly evokes compassion for the defeated enemy. It begins and ends with Persian grief, expressed ungloatingly, as genuine sorrow:

> here, each Persian wife,
> Longing for him she sped
> Armed to the fierce campaign,
> Sprinkling her empty bed
> With tender tears in vain,
> Weeps out her lonely life. (p. 126)

The Persian characters are not presented as barbarian warmongers. King Darius, who appears as a ghost, is a wise and serene character, even though the historical Darius would have been anyone's first choice to exemplify Persian brutality. As David Rosenbloom remarks in his study of the play, its account of Persian history suggests that Xerxes's militarism is aberrant rather than typical (pp. 143–4). Christopher Collard, editor of the Oxford edition, notes that despite the play's emphasis on Persian extravagance and excess, its tragic dynamics engage the audience's pity (p. xxiv). To see the play as both depicting the hubris of the Persians and expressing Greek triumphalism would surely be contradictory. More likely, when the Persian queen says

> When waves of trouble burst on us, each new
> event

> Fills us with terror; but when Fortune's wind
>    blows soft
> We think to enjoy the same fair weather all our
>    lives (p. 139)

the Athenian audience is being reminded that their own triumphalism might itself be hubristic, a point that assumes a continuity of experience between Susa and Athens. The first play in the canon of world theatre demonstrates the cosmopolitan ethos that can arise from international antagonism.

## Universals and theatre

The cosmopolitan principle that all human beings are members of a single moral community is not without its critics. Imperialists in the nineteenth century and neoconservatives in the twenty-first have rampaged across the globe in the belief they know the universal truths of humanity, determined to bring civilization or democracy to the rest of the world. 'Universalism' – a belief that the same principles are valid for everyone – has become tainted by association.

This has manifested as mistrust of claims to universality in the theatre. Complicite – formerly Théâtre de Complicité – have been described as 'the most cosmopolitan theatre group in Britain' (Kustow, p. xii), and though this description may refer specifically to their international casts and international touring, their piece *Mnemonic* (Lawrence Batley Theatre, Huddersfield, 1999) also gives audiences a chance to experience their own cosmopolitan connectedness. At the beginning of the show, Simon McBurney – the show's director and also one of its actors – addresses us directly, asking us to find under our seats a bag containing a blindfold and a leaf. He instructs us to put on the blindfold and feel the leaf, with its branching structure of veins, as a kind of family tree: us as the stalk, and our ancestors the veins. He asks us to imagine the huge and growing breadth of the tree at its tallest as we go further back through the generations. Eventually, he explains, we reach a point where there are more people in all this audience's family trees than there actually were people in the world, with the implication that everyone in the theatre is part of a single family.

Having started with a deduction of our common humanity, the performance itself puts flesh on those statistical bones, introducing us to several rather particular stories of European journeys and the search for roots. An image of our common ancestry is given in the strand that deals with the (real) discovery in 1991 of the 'Ice Man', a 5,300-year-old corpse mummified by the icy conditions in the mountains between Italy and Austria. We watch an international group of scientists trying to overcome jurisdictional disputes and other cultural and interpretive differences to reconstruct the Ice Man's final moments, until finally we see them: a wooden chair is taken apart and turned into a puppet representation of the Ice Man, whom we see making his final journey before lying down to die. Once again, we are introduced to an image that is both general and specific; it is one particular figure dying over five millennia in the past, but in its representation in puppet form, its particular human features are removed and it is allowed to stand in for everyone. As the show comes to an end, a physical sequence has each member of the cast rolling across a dissecting table, suggesting a continuity between the Ice Man and the whole of humanity.

In an article published shortly after the premiere, Helen Freshwater argued that in employing such images *Mnemonic* points a way beyond the unstable relativism of some contemporary scholarship by locating the body as 'an ethical base' (p. 218), a kind of historical constant that can ground a sense of our common humanity. Janelle Reinelt was, in contrast, uncomfortable with the show's 'return to universalism' and disputed the idea that 'all humans [are] essentially similar in their travels, their struggles to survive, their bodiliness', which both illegitimately extends Europe's self-image across the world and suggests – anti-politically – that nothing ever does or can change (p. 376). Jen Harvie, in *Staging the UK*, offers a midway position, arguing that *Mnemonic*'s 'attempted universalising can simultaneously draw attention to *both* the benefits that Freshwater identifies and the problems that Reinelt raises', but she also believes that the production's universalizing extends only to the frontiers of Europe, offering not a sense of humanity but only a shared European heritage (p. 141). Universalism remains controversial.

For that reason, some theatre scholars have tried to qualify cosmopolitanism to remove its universalist taint: Helen Gilbert and Jacqueline Lo, in *Performance and Cosmopolitics*, cite concepts such as 'discrepant cosmopolitanism', 'rooted cosmopolitanism', 'postcolonial cosmopolitanism', 'universalism plus difference', and the 'polymorphic universal' (pp. 4–6); Paul Rae, in 'Where Is the Cosmopolitan Stage?', cites 'cosmopolitan vernacular', 'cosmopolitanism from below', 'critical cosmopolitanism', 'cosmofeminism', and other concepts (p. 10). All these terms attempt to adapt cosmopolitanism to reflect the importance of global diversity.

Although I believe that such attempts to finesse cosmopolitanism come from a justifiable concern for the marginalization of different cultures, identities, practices, and positions of power, I think they miss the point. More important, they risk obscuring precisely what is so radical about cosmopolitanism. For one thing, it is easy to overstate the significance and extent of diversity. Although there are huge differences of cultural practice and belief in the world, is wrongful imprisonment, or torture, or murder, or rape less wrong in Burma than it is in Boston? Perpetrators of such acts sometimes try to defend them on the grounds of cultural difference, but if diversity is all then nothing can ever be criticized and ethics – and with it, politics – is nothing. For the cosmopolitan, it is important that the oppressed can appeal to universal rights beyond the level of the state.

Second, the critics of cosmopolitanism are often forced to adopt tacitly cosmopolitan arguments. As we've seen, the claim is made that cosmopolitans sometimes dress their own principles up as universal ones, imposing Western (or male, or white, or heterosexual, etc.) attitudes on everyone else. And why is that a bad thing? Surely, it is bad, not because it's too universalising, but because, by failing to respect important differences in the world, it is not universalising *enough*.

The claim that we should respect cultural differences is — as I suggested in my discussion of localization — a universalist ethical principle. What cosmopolitanism's critics are really talking about is uniformity, which is indeed an unattractive quality to impose on the world, and it is something of which globalization is guilty, not cosmopolitanism.

But I don't just want to defend cosmopolitanism. I want to go further: to suggest that cosmopolitanism is in fact a radical opponent of globalization. Once I have done that, I will show how its principles may be embodied in the theatre.

## Cosmopolitanism versus globalization

Kant's cosmopolitanism is grounded in his moral philosophy, and here is the source of its radical antagonism to globalization. In Kantian ethics, the right action in any given situation is not a matter of weighing up outcomes: the rightness of an action is given by the rational processes of our own minds. Kant starts from a famous, if puzzling, observation in moral philosophy: that despite living in what we know to be a causal universe (where every event is the result of a previous event, stretching back endlessly through time), this causality doesn't feel as if it applies to us. In other words, when I am faced with a choice, I feel the choice really is mine to make and is not already causally determined in the way that the bending of a branch on a windy day is purely the effect of the wind, which is in turn the effect of changes of atmospheric pressure, which is the effect of the variable heating of the earth, and so on.

If our will is free in this way, then we are potentially able to resist external pressures (bribery, threats, and so on) and also internal ones (greed, cowardice, and so on). We know this because people are capable of acting 'selflessly' and not purely to satisfy their desires. We are not merely animals, led by instinct and biological programming. As Hamlet puts it, puzzling over the wellsprings of action: 'What is a man/ If his chief good and market of his time / Be but to sleep and feed? A beast, no more' (p. 363).

What this means is that our free will is free of self-interest. Kant distinguishes between two kinds of requirement to do something: hypothetical imperatives and categorical imperatives. Hypothetical imperatives have the form 'If you want *x*, you should do *y*'. For example, if you want to satisfy your hunger, you should eat some food. The requirement to act is conditional on some project or desire. Categorical imperatives are *unconditional*; they take the form 'You should do *y*', regardless of your projects or desires. For example, 'You must not commit murder' can be described as a categorical imperative because it does not depend on any further end. Categorical imperatives are moral; hypothetical ones are non-moral.

For Kant, categorical imperatives derive from our reason. When I contemplate acting in a certain way, my impersonal reason asks whether the principle on which I intend to act could coherently be one that *everyone* could act upon. For example, suppose you could persuade someone to lend you money if you promise to repay it, but you know you're leaving the country and will never see them again. Reason asks: could *everyone* act on this principle ('I can break my promise if it's to my advantage')? It is clear that they could not, because if they did, no one would trust anyone's promises, and you wouldn't gain any advantage by making a false one.

Globalization is driven by a hypothetical imperative: to make money. If you want to make money, you should invest in new machinery; if you want to make money, you should pretend to be more environmentally sensitive than you are; if you want to make money, you should transfer the manufacture of your clothes to a South-East Asian sweatshop, and so on. As we've seen, some claim that capitalism tends to produce moral behaviour because if businesspeople don't act honestly and fairly, their customers won't come back and they will go out of business; it is therefore in the interests of business to act ethically. The Kantian response to this claim is that even if this were true – and it isn't – their behaviour only *resembles* moral action; it is not actually moral.

To clarify this curious idea, imagine two friends of yours are each offered $50,000 to kill you. Both of them reject the offer: the first because she thinks it's wrong to commit murder, the second because she might get caught and the fee is not enough. Which one is acting ethically? Even though the result is the same, I'm sure you'd agree that the first person is acting ethically and the second is not. Similarly, if businesspeople decide to be honest because they think that will make them more money, they're not really being 'honest' in any ethically satisfying way. In their book *Investing in West End Theatrical Productions*, Philippe Carden and Bee Huntley consider how you judge whether a production is likely to make you money. One tip is to mention the proposed cast to your children and look into their eyes to see whether you can detect flickers of recognition and excitement (p. 72). It's a good example of the market's ethically distorted imperatives that it requires you to look into the eyes of your children as a source of market-sensitive information.

Already, I hope, you can see how cosmopolitan is distinct from the ethics governing globalization. Two other aspects are worth underlining. First, the categorical imperative is founded on *absolute equality of consideration of every person in the world*: in making a moral judgement we invoke the global community of all persons. Our ethical judgements, therefore, play themselves out at a global level. Second, the categorical imperative is *a priori*; that is, its commands are logically prior to our experience of the world, which means it has a prior authority to the hypothetical imperatives of global capital. Globalization is unprecedented in the range and depth of its penetration of the world, but our ethical judgements have always got there first.

## Theatre and cosmopolitanism

What role can the theatre play in this? How can – how *does* – theatre and performance help us experience our place in the cosmopolitan community? There are several ways in which the theatre perhaps rehearses the nature of our ethical obligations. Acting a character involves a level of imaginative engagement with another (fictional) person, a determination to occupy and understand that person's actions, whether that is psychologically or socially. Acting might itself be considered a valuable rehearsal for the ethical principle of universal equivalence between all people. (We need to be cautious here: Frederick Winslow Taylor, introduced above as the inventor of scientific management, was apparently an enthusiastic amateur actor in his younger days, but that didn't seem to stop him turning the industrial worker into little more than a machine.)

There may be something distinctly ethical in the position of the audience. First, their identification with characters on stage – often kinds of people that we would not ordinarily encounter –perhaps prepares the way for such identifications outside the theatre. Second, the theatre often presents situations in a way that foregrounds the ethical dilemmas involved in them, and here of course we would include plays that address very directly the problems of globalization. Third, and perhaps more interesting, the audience's relation to itself can be an unusual experience of commonality. Anyone who has seen a particularly good piece of theatre will be familiar with the audience becoming one, unified in the intensity of their attention or in the infectiousness of their common laughter. A cosmopolitan ethical principle is founded in both the autonomy of the individual will *and* the universal community of beings, and in a theatre audience we can have a very sharp sense of being both ourselves *and* a part of a larger unity.

Earlier, I mentioned Mark Ravenhill's claim that the structures of conventional naturalistic playwriting are no longer adequate to the new realities of a globalizing world. Perhaps, too, cosmopolitanism demands new theatrical and performance forms. Baz Kershaw, in *The Radical in Performance*, describes a performance installation by the

Colombian company Taller de Investigación de la Imagen Dramática called *The Labyrinth*, which he visited in Bangor, Wales, in October 1996. The form of the installation, as its title suggests, was an extensive maze, into which, one at a time, audience members were invited to go. Much of the maze was very dark, and it was so large that you quickly lost your bearings, both in space and in time. At moments corridors opened into chambers, each with a different performer inside. The environments were sensual, charged; you alternated between exhilaration and fear. The darkness and disorientation made you intensely aware of yourself and, by depriving you of some of the usual tools you use to situate yourself in the world, required that you *trust* the performers in an unusually direct way. This mixture of self-awareness and trust, says Kershaw, offered participants 'an extraordinary sense of the power of human mutuality' (p. 208) and an intense sense of our interconnectedness in the world.

Stan's Cafe's installation *Of All the People in All the World* (Warwick Arts Centre, Coventry, 2003) has a quite different set of artistic values to *The Labyrinth*: it's witty rather than intense, coolly empirical rather than emotionally fraught. The show, which has toured the world, is a series of exhibits that represent the people of the world, divided up into various categories, using a grain of rice to denote one person. When you enter the exhibition, you see a series of piles of rice, each with its own label. Some of the piles are very large ('The Population of India'); others are very small ('People Who Have Walked on the Moon'). Some of the piles plainly represent important statistics about the current state of the world ('The World's Refugees'), and others are amusingly frivolous ('Extras Involved in the Making of *The Lord of the Rings* Trilogy'). The version seen at the Wagenhalle, Stuttgart, in 2005, was the largest yet. Using 104 tons of rice, it managed to represent the entire population of the world in one room. The show addresses one of the concerns raised about cosmopolitanism, that we can't meaningfully imagine the population of the world – because our imaginations don't work at a high enough resolution to be able to hold the individual and the whole at the same time. *Of All the People in All the World* feeds the cosmopolitan imagination, giving us new ways of grasping the enormity of the world, and the imagination feeds our perception of the exhibits, as we invest – in a somewhat theatrical way – the blank uniformity of each rice pile with personality and significance.

One thing links *The Labyrinth* and *Of All the People in All the World* with *Mnemonic*, which I discussed earlier: a certain rebalancing of sight and imagination. *Mnemonic*'s blindfold and *The Labyrinth*'s darkness have an affinity with the imaginative and non-literal connections we are required to make between the world and Stan's Cafe's piles of rice. There is a good reason for this, which I think lies in the requirement that we stop seeing the world as it happens to be and start seeing it instead as it might be. What we *see* tends to be local; what we *imagine*, as Arjun Appadurai says, operates 'beyond the boundaries of the nation' (p. 8). In this final section of the book, I want to suggest that the theatre has a number of important formal complexities that make it particularly suitable for developing and sustaining the ethical imagination; put another way, the theatre's formal modes tend towards cosmopolitanism.

Joseph de Maistre, the eighteenth-century conservative, mocked the French Revolution's Declaration of the Rights of Man on the grounds that 'in the course of my life I have seen Frenchmen, Italians, Russians, etc.; I even know, thanks to Montesquieu, that one can be Persian; but as for *man*, I declare I have never met one in my life' (quoted in Appiah, p. 111). Perhaps he never went to the theatre. Although we cannot *see* someone who is only an 'object of moral worth' (that's what 'man' means in this context), we can imagine him or her, and we can represent him or her in our imagination and in the theatre. If someone – perhaps the same person who was trying to have you assassinated a few pages back – were to offer you $50,000 to kill the next person who walked through the door, you might (if you were Joseph de Maistre) say, 'I cannot know, because I have never seen a "person"', or you could say, 'No thanks, killing people is wrong.' The latter reaction – which, quite honestly, I hope is yours – seems to me entirely plausible and meaningful, and it proceeds on no information about the target other than his or her personhood. And we can do that in the theatre. If a stage direction reads 'A person enters', the playwright has created a being with no other identifiable features than his or her personhood.

Maistre might object that although the general person might be conceptually possible on the page, in production the person who enters will be not a general person but a particular person. Three things may interrupt this descent to the particular. The first is that the theatre can create characters who are less particular than real people tend to be. Over the course of his writing life, Beckett's dramatic characters became more and more abstracted: from the odd but proper names Vladimir, Estragon, and Pozzo in *Waiting for Godot* (Théâtre de Babylone, Paris, 1953), to the more formalized Winnie and Willie in *Happy Days* (Cherry Lane Theater, New York, 1961), through to the reduction of character to markers of gender – W1, W2, M – in *Play* (Ulmer Theater, Ulm-Donau, 1963) and the bodily truncation to 'Mouth' in *Not I* (Lincoln Center, 1972).

This gradual evaporation of singularity has been particularly characteristic of playwriting in the era of globalization: Sarah Kane followed the Beckettian trajectory by moving from Ian and Cate in *Blasted* to A, B, C, and M in *Crave* (Paines Plough, 1998), and in her final play, *4.48 Psychosis* (Royal Court Theatre Upstairs, 2000), no characters are indicated at all. In this she was influenced by Martin Crimp's play *Attempts on Her Life* (Royal Court Theatre Upstairs, 1997), whose seventeen scenes – Crimp calls them 'scenarios', perhaps to highlight their provisional status – are made up of lines of dialogue unassigned to a character, requiring each production to distribute the lines as it sees fit, and thus re-create the scenes anew. What connects these disparate scenes is the name Anne and its variants – the name of a (probably) offstage figure who at times seems to be a fun-loving teenager and at others a brutal terrorist. Anne is both over- and under-specified, making her virtually impossible to place as an individual. The name Anne suggests the indefinite article, and one of the play's many achievements is to produce a vivid indefinite character.

Second, in the theatre we often engage with fictional characters. Fictional characters behave very differently than real people, not in the ordinary sense that they tend to be more heroic or more villainous but in the way they present themselves to us. Even if the characters are embodied by real people, any reasonably competent theatregoer knows that not everything that is true of the performers we see in front of us is true of the characters they are playing. In 1997, I saw a production of Chekhov's *The Seagull* at the Donmar in London. Before the show we were informed that Mark Bazeley, the actor playing Konstantin, had hurt his leg and would be performing on crutches; I therefore understood that although the person in front of me was on crutches, Konstantin was not – which illustrates that just because an actor is necessarily particularized it does not follow that the character must be too. The relationship between actor and character is not a literal one: when the programme says Mark Bazeley is Konstantin, it is not expressing a relationship of identity (water is $H_2O$) or of a subject to a predicate (water is wet). It does not demand that Mark Bazeley is *like* Konstantin or vice versa. After all, if a chair or a grain of rice can 'play' a person, the theatrical relation clearly is not essentially one of resemblance. When we say Mark Bazeley is Konstantin, we are saying something like Mark Bazeley *is a metaphor for* Konstantin. This metaphorical relation affects every element of theatrical meaning: objects on stage may resemble the objects they are representing, but they don't have to.

This is connected to my third thought about the ability of theatre to create non-specific characters: there is always a gap between a play and its production. Whenever we watch a play, even if we are watching it for the first and only time, we are aware that it *could* be staged differently. Una Chaudhuri writes that 'the intrinsic doubleness of theater, the fact that it produces and reproduces something that is prior to it (the script), makes for an inherent displacement and temporalization. ... Putting its material into play again and again, from rehearsal to rehearsal and then from night to night, the theatre is a space of creative reinscription, a space where meaning, like deterritorialized identity, is not merely made but remade, negotiated out of silence, stasis, and incomprehension' (pp. 173–4). The play in performance has a dual structure: we both watch what we see and imagine it differently. This is notably different from the localized form of theatre – community and site-specific work – which demands that what we see could not be done differently, because it has no meaning anywhere else. In the gaps between the play and the performance lies a cosmopolitan politics.

This structure is best exemplified in a show which is not really a play at all. Forced Entertainment's *Dirty Work* (Phoenix Arts, Leicester, 1998) is performed by two actors, and the text they perform is a long description of a performance. The show they describe is five acts long and contains both classic narrative elements ('A woman writes a letter and delivers it to the wrong address. Another woman reads it by mistake and so becomes embroiled in someone else's unpleasant story', p. 4) and preposterous, impossible moments of spectacular, epic bravado ('Aeroplanes leave vapour trails in the sky, writing amusing messages as they loop beneath the clouds', p. 7). The show places enormous, comically excessive demands on our ability to imagine the play that is taking place, but in doing so simply foregrounds what we normally do when we go to see a play, because, in theatre as in a globalized world, we always need to remember that what *is* is not what *must be*.

Spanish director Rodrigo Garcia's *The Story of Ronald, the Clown of McDonald's* (La Carnicería Teatro, 2002) is a scabrous piece of theatre that begins with small-scale monologues which dissolve into an argument, then violence, and then a massive food fight, until the entire stage is filled with the overpowering sights and smells of one of globalization's most famous products: McDonald's food. The performance is both viscerally, sensuously direct in its engagement with globalization and wittily oblique in its playful refusal to address its subject matter through editorial commentary; in this way, it holds the power of McDonald's aesthetically suspended as an object in question.

This same drive towards generalizing character, allowing us to imagine people in general, transforms space. Several recent plays and performance texts work through a kind of de-territorializing ambiguity. *Stoning Mary* by debbie tucker green (Royal Court/Plymouth Drum, 2005) is 'set in the country it is performed in' and 'all characters are white' (p. 2), though the three scenarios that are described – a couple deciding which of them will use their one allocated AIDS treatment, a woman condemned to death by stoning, and the return of a child soldier – are more readily associated with the continent of Africa. At the Royal Court, then, the play appeared to be taking place both in Africa and in the UK. Martin Crimp's short performance text *Advice to Iraqi Women* (Royal Court, 2003), presented in the run-up to the invasion of Iraq, is a list of stern prohibitions about the protection of children: 'Lock sheds. Lock garden chemicals out of reach. Secure hoses. If you have a greenhouse with seedlings in it, keep the child away. When your child is in the pool, screaming in the pool, supervise it at all times, and don't let it burn.' The advice seems to imagine a well-to-do English suburban lifestyle and to have little to do with the threatened Iraqis, except for a series of darkly ambiguous resonances in the language ('Your house is a minefield', 'Your house is a potential war zone'), which, in another piece of impossible geography, place the play simultaneously in the UK and in Iraq.

Caryl Churchill's *Far Away* (Royal Court Theatre Upstairs, 2000) combines many of these features. It falls into three parts: in the first, a young girl, Joan, questions her aunt about some disturbing sights she has seen the night before; in the second, Joan, now grown up, works making elaborate hats alongside a co-worker while outside the country is holding show trials and executing the guilty; in the third act, a full-scale war of all against all has broken out across the world, and, as the play unfolds, we discover it has drawn in animals, birds, insects, plants, and even the elements themselves. Joan reports back from her arduous journey across the battle lines:

> there was one killed by coffee or one killed by pins, they were killed by heroin, petrol, chainsaws, hairspray, bleach, foxgloves, the smell of smoke was where we were burning the grass that wouldn't serve. The Bolivians are working with gravity, that's a secret so as not to spread alarm. But we're getting further with noise and there's thousands dead of light in Madagascar. Who's going to mobilise darkness and silence? that's what I wondered in the night. (p. 159)

The play does not indicate place except in its move from the domestic to the national to the global. In the turmoil of international allegiances in the last act, the play presents national differences as moral absurdities. What the play's cosmopolitan movement does is render the moral significance of 'far away' meaningless.

Time is the last formal aspect of theatre to have been dramatically altered by the perspectival shifts of globalization. Aristotle, in the *Poetics*, declared that the length of a play should permit you to take it in as a single thought. Several contemporary theatre-makers have defied Aristotle's advice. Robert Lepage's *The Dragons Trilogy* (Théâtre Repère, Quebec City, 1985) is five-and-a-half hours long; his *Lipsynch* (Barbican, London, 2008) is nine hours long.

Durational live art performances work to create new modes of spectatorship, such as La Ribot's *Laughing Hole* (Art Unlimited, Basel, 2006), in which a series of performers, laughing constantly, tape words to the wall of the performance space, and Forced Entertainment's *Quizoola!* (ICA, 1996), in which two performers in bad clown make-up ask each other a series of alternately banal, stupid, and serious questions; both shows last around six hours. Attending all the parts of Societas Raffaello Sanzio's *Tragedia Endogonidia* took three years and demanded travel to ten European cities. From November 2002 to November 2003, Suzan-Lori Parks wrote a short play every day, and performances of the resulting *365 Plays* were scattered across 600 different US theatre groups. In April 2008, Mark Ravenhill's *Shoot/Get Treasure/Repeat* comprised sixteen different play texts, which were performed at six different locations across London. Howard Barker's preposterous and brilliant *The Ecstatic Bible* was seen at the Adelaide Festival in 2000 in a cut-down version; even so it ran to six hours.

In Barker's theatrical manifesto *Arguments for a Theatre*, he declares with characteristic confidence:

> Plays are much too short. The manager likes the short play, it fits his wage bills. The writer of short plays thinks 'they will grow impatient with me!' Because truth is complex, art is also complex. It cannot be smashed to fit the timetable of trains.
>
> One day a play will be written for which men and women will miss a day's work.

It is likely this play will itself be experienced
as work. (p. 24)

A long piece of theatre is disruptive in a number of ways.
It overflows the spaces usually allocated by our culture as
leisure time; it de-naturalizes our mode of spectatorship and
forces us to make conscious decisions about it. (Is everything
equally important? What structures do we impose on theatre and performance from convention and familiarity with
the form?) As such it makes us ask questions about the value
of the theatre, sets it up as a rival to work, with its hypothetical imperatives and means-end logic. What we discover is
that the theatre and work have very different kinds of value.
Most people work in order to get paid; often we go to the
theatre for no other reason than the theatre itself.

Kant, in his *Critique of the Power of Judgment*, wrote
that beauty is 'a symbol of morality' (p. 225 [5:351]). What
Kant means in this curious phrase is that our experience of
beauty – and this term should be considered in its broadest
sense to include all kinds of positive aesthetic valuation –
has particular affinities with our experience of morality.
First, the way we value art is somewhat like the way we
value other people. We value both for their own sake and
not as a means to an end. (If I value my friend *only* because
she lends me money when I need it, you might reasonably
conclude I don't have a proper appreciation of friendship; if
I go to the theatre *only* because I think it will impress my
workmates, you might reasonably conclude I don't have a
proper appreciation of art.)

Second, for Kant, when we experience artistic beauty, that particular kind of mental expansiveness, profundity, and excitement – fill in your own description of experiencing good theatre here – is produced by two faculties of the mind in a kind of harmonious free play. That is, our sensory experience of the artwork (the imagination) and the bank of concepts that we carry with us (the understanding) are engaged, but without needing to finally determine the meaning of what we are experiencing. Hence, when you see a play, the literal facts of what is happening (a few actors walking around a stage shouting) do not exhaust the meaning of the experience; everything seems additionally charged with significance, and the more artistically satisfying the theatre is, the more inexhaustible this significance feels. What we are encountering here is the universal structure of the mind in an unusually pure form: in aesthetic experience we momentarily disengage from the particular set of concepts that each of us has and we experience our common humanity. And just as art evokes our common humanity, so does morality. Indeed, cosmopolitanism is prepared for by both art and morality.

## Conclusion

There has been a tendency among politically minded theatre critics to believe that theatre is at its most political when it is explicitly representing political situations, characters, and events. A political play about globalization might therefore be a play set in a global corporation, with the CEO as the protagonist forced to confront a dilemma about whether to export the company's jobs to a low-wage country. Characters representing the shareholders, the investment bank, and the unions could be brought in to engage in lively dialectics with the agonizing boss. Perhaps, for added spice and a human angle, the CEO's brother-in-law could work for the company and be at risk of losing his job. Maybe a good play could be written on this topic, and it might excite the feelings of its audience on all sides of the debate.

I hope I have shown, though, that globalization requires a theatrical response that is different in kind from the political topics of earlier generations. Globalization's power is so immense and its scale so far outstrips our current governmental structures that we have to create new forms of international association, new forms of governance, new forms of global civil society that will give shape and force to our humanity and our responsibility. In doing so we will need to draw on theatre's particular modes of production – its gaps and complexities, its striving for beauty and grace and ambiguity and metaphor – to offer an arsenal of experiences that can help us to grasp the everywhere and the everyone. There is an ethical impulse in the theatre's aesthetics, regardless of how globalization may wax and wane, whose singular moments of beauty allow us to glimpse the breadth and intensity of the cosmopolitan community.

# further reading

The literature on globalization is enormous, but Steger, Waters, and Ellwood are decent starting points. Lechner and Boli is a good collection of important essays, as is Held and McGrew. Still the most powerful account of globalization, in my opinion, is *The Communist Manifesto*, which is contained in its entirety in Marx's *Selected Writings*, edited by David McLennan, a compendious single-volume selection that is more than enough Marx for most people. The book that to me best sets out the philosophical issues raised by globalization is Singer's *One World*, even if I don't agree with all of his conclusions. You can find good, succinct statements about the value of a market economy on both sides of the debate in Butler (pro) and Harvey (anti). The debates over cosmopolitanism are covered well in Archibugi's collection. If you are interested in Kant, Wood's book is a good, clear introduction, while Bohman and Lutz-Bachmann's collection is more directly focused on interpreting his cosmopolitical ideas. Ridout's *Theatre & Ethics* – in this series – is a brilliantly compendious and pugnacious synthesis of various ethical systems and their implications for theatre.

Surprisingly little has been written on theatre and globalization. There have been two special issues of journals dedicated to this subject: *Theatre Journal* 57.3 (2005, ed. Jean Graham-Jones) and *Contemporary Theatre Review* 16.1 (2006, eds. Jen Harvie and Dan Rebellato). If you can track these down, they are both worth reading. A great deal of interest is contained in Bharucha, Svich, Wickstrom, and Lonergan. I'll risk accusations of vanity and mention a couple of my own pieces, one from 2006 discussing the spatial indeterminacy of playwriting and its relation to globalization, the second, from 2007, tracing the move away from 'state of the nation plays' towards a formal reflection of the global. There are some very good resources on theatre and cosmopolitanism, especially Gilbert and Lo, and the articles by Rae and Chaudhuri.

Aeschylus. *Prometheus Bound and Other Plays*. Ed. Philip Vellacott. Harmondsworth, UK: Penguin, 1961.

————. *Persians and Other Plays*. Ed. Christopher Collard. Oxford: Oxford UP, 2009.

Anderson, Sarah, and John Cavanagh. *Top 200: The Rise of Corporate Global Power*. Washington DC: Institute for Policy Studies, 2000.

Appadurai, Arjun. *Modernity at Large: Cultural Dimensions of Globalization*. Public Worlds. Minneapolis: U of Minnesota P, 1996.

Appiah, Kwame Anthony. 'Cosmopolitan Patriots.' *Cosmopolitics: Thinking and Feeling Beyond the Nation*. Ed. Pheng Cheah and Bruce Robbins. Minneapolis: U of Minnesota P, 1998. 91–114.

Archibugi, Daniele, ed. *Debating Cosmopolitanism*. London: Verso, 2003.

Artaud, Antonin. *Collected Works: Volume Four*. Trans. Victor Corti. London: John Calder, 1974. [Includes *The Theatre and Its Double*]

Auslander, Philip. *Liveness: Performance in a Mediatized Culture*. 2nd ed. London: Routledge, 2008.

Barber, Benjamin R. *Jihad vs. McWorld*. New York: Times Books, 1995.

Barker, Harley Granville. *Plays: One*. London: Methuen, 1993.

Barker, Howard. *Arguments for a Theatre*. 3rd ed. Manchester: Manchester UP, 1997.

Batchelor, Ray. *Henry Ford: Mass Production, Modernism and Design*. Manchester: Manchester UP, 1994.

Bello, Walden. *Deglobalization: Ideas for a New World Economy*. 2nd ed. London: Zed, 2004.

Bennett, Susan. 'Theatre/Tourism.' *Theatre Journal* 57.3 (2005): 407–28.

Bharucha, Rustom. *The Politics of Cultural Practice: Thinking Through Theatre in an Age of Globalization*. London: Athlone, 2000.

Black, Edwin. *IBM and the Holocaust: The Strategic Alliance between Nazi Germany and America's Most Powerful Corporation*. New York: Crown, 2001.

Bohman, James, and Matthias Lutz-Bachmann, eds. *Perpetual Peace: Essays on Kant's Cosmopolitan Ideal*. Cambridge, MA, and London: MIT Press, 1997.

Bulwer-Lytton, Edward. *Money*. *Nineteenth Century Plays*. Ed. George Rowell. 2nd ed. Oxford: Oxford UP, 1972.

Burston, Jonathan. 'Theatre Space as Virtual Place: Audio Technology, the Reconfigured Singing Body, and the Megamusical.' *Popular Music* 17.2 (1998): 205–18.

———. 'Spectacle, Synergy and Megamusicals: The Global-Industrialisation of the Live-Entertainment Economy.' *Media Organisations in Society*. Ed. James Curran. London: Arnold, 2000. 69–83.

Butler, Eamonn. *The Best Book on the Market: How to Stop Worrying and Love the Free Economy*. Chichester, UK: Capstone, 2008.

Carden, Philippe, and Bee Huntley. *Investing in West End Theatrical Productions: How to Be an Angel*. London: Robert Hale, 1992.

Castellucci, Claudia, et al. *The Theatre of Societas Raffaello Sanzio*. Abingdon, UK: Routledge, 2007.

Chaudhuri, Una. 'Theater and Cosmopolitanism: New Stories, Old Stages.' *Cosmopolitan Geographies: New Locations in Literature and*

*Culture*. Ed. Vinay Dharwadker. New York: Routledge, 2000. 171–95.

Churchill, Caryl. *Plays: 4*. London: Nick Hern, 2008.

Cohen-Cruz, Jan. *Local Acts: Community-Based Performance in the United States*. New Brunswick, NJ: Rutgers UP, 2005.

Crimp, Martin. 'Advice to Iraqi Women.' *Guardian* 10 April 2003. 14 September 2008 <www.guardian.co.uk/stage/2003/apr/10/theatre. artsfeatures1>.

Dobbs, Michael. 'Ford and GM Scrutinized for Alleged Nazi Collaboration.' *Washington Post* 30 November 1998: A01.

Ellwood, Wayne. *No-Nonsense Guide to Globalization*. London: Verso–New Internationalist, 2001.

Forced Entertainment. *Dirty Work*. Sheffield: Forced Entertainment, 1998.

Freshwater, Helen. 'The Ethics of Indeterminacy: Theatre de Complicite's "Mnemonic".' *New Theatre Quarterly* 17.3 (2001): 212–18.

Friedman, Thomas L. *The Lexus and the Olive Tree*. New York: Farrar, Straus, Giroux, 1999.

Gabor, Andrea. *The Capitalist Philosophers: The Geniuses of Modern Business – Their Lives, Times and Ideas*. Chichester, UK, and New York: Wiley, 2000.

Galsworthy, John. *Five Plays*. London: Methuen, 1984.

Giddens, Anthony. *The Consequences of Modernity*. Cambridge: Polity Press, 1990.

Gilbert, Helen, and Jacqueline Lo. *Performance and Cosmopolitics: Cross-cultural Transactions in Australasia*. Basingstoke, UK: Palgrave, 2007.

Graham-Jones, Jean. 'Editorial Comment: Theorizing Globalization Through Theatre.' *Theatre Journal* 57.3 (2005): viii–xvi.

green, debbie tucker. *Stoning Mary*. London: Nick Hern, 2005.

Greenpeace. 'Contamination in Paulínia by Aldrin, Dieldrin, Endrin and Other Toxic Chemicals Produced and Disposed of by Shell Chemicals of Brazil.' Greenpeace International. April 2001. 18 November 2008 <www.greenpeace.org/raw/content/international/press/reports/ contamination-in-paul-nia-by-a.pdf>.

Habermas, Jürgen. *The Postnational Constellation: Political Essays*. Cambridge: Polity, 2001.

Hare, David. *Obedience, Struggle & Revolt: Lectures on Theatre*. London: Faber & Faber, 2005.

Harvey, David. *A Brief History of Neoliberalism*. Oxford: Oxford UP, 2005.

Harvie, Jen. *Staging the UK*. Manchester: Manchester UP, 2005.

Held, David, and Anthony McGrew, eds. *The Global Transformations Reader: An Introduction to the Globalization Debate*. 2nd ed. Cambridge: Polity, 2003.

Henderson, David. *Misguided Virtue: False Notions of Corporate Social Responsibility*. London: Institute of Economic Affairs, 2001.

Hilton, Steve, and Giles Gibbons. *Good Business: Your World Needs You*. London: Texere, 2002.

Hines, Colin. *Localization: A Global Manifesto*. London: Earthscan, 2000.

Hoffman, Jens, and Joan Jonas. *Perform*. London: Thames & Hudson, 2005.

Huntington, Samuel P. *The Clash of Civilizations and the Remaking of World Order*. London: Free Press, 2002.

Kane, Sarah. *Complete Plays*. London: Methuen, 2001.

Kanigel, Robert. *The One Best Way: Frederick Winslow Taylor and the Enigma of Efficiency*. London: Little, Brown, 1997.

Kant, Immanuel. *Practical Philosophy*. Ed. and trans. Mary J. Gregor. Cambridge: Cambridge UP, 1996.

———. *Critique of the Power of Judgment*. Cambridge: Cambridge UP, 2000.

———. *Anthropology, History, and Education*. Trans. Mary Gregor et al. Ed. Günter Zöller and Robert B Louden. Cambridge: Cambridge UP, 2007.

Kaye, Nick. *Art into Theatre: Performance, Interviews and Documents*. Amsterdam: Harwood Academic, 1996.

Kershaw, Baz. *The Radical in Performance: Between Brecht and Baudrillard*. London: Routledge, 1999.

Kingsnorth, Paul. *One No, Many Yeses: Journey to the Heart of the Global Resistance Movement*. London: Simon & Schuster, 2003.

Kustow, Michael. *theatre@risk*. 2nd ed. London: Methuen, 2001.

Lapierre, Dominique, and Javier Moro. *Five Past Midnight in Bhopal*. London: Scribner, 2001.

Lechner, Frank J., and John Boli, eds. *The Globalization Reader*. 3rd ed. Oxford: Blackwell, 2007.

Lillo, George. *The London Merchant*. Ed. William H McBurney. Lincoln: U of Nebraska P, 1965.

Lonergan, Patrick. *Theatre and Globalization: Irish Drama in the Celtic Tiger Age*. Basingstoke, UK: Palgrave, 2008.

Maddison, Angus. *The World Economy: A Millennial Perspective*. Paris: Development Centre of the Organisation for Economic Co-operation and Development, 2001.

Marx, Karl. *Grundrisse: Foundation of the Critique of Political Economy*. Harmondsworth, UK: Penguin–New Left Review, 1973.

———. *Selected Writings*. Ed. David McLennan. 2nd ed. Oxford: Oxford UP, 2000.

Morley, Sheridan, and Ruth Leon. *Hey, Mr Producer! The Musical World of Cameron Mackintosh*. London: Weidenfeld & Nicolson, 1998.

Polybius. *The Rise of the Roman Empire*. Trans. Ian Scott-Kilvert. Ed. Frank William Walbank. Harmondsworth, UK: Penguin, 1979.

Rae, Paul. 'Where Is the Cosmopolitan Stage?' *Contemporary Theatre Review* 16.1 (2006): 8–22.

Ravenhill, Mark. 'Me, My iBook, and Writing in America.' *Contemporary Theatre Review* 16.1 (2006): 131–8.

Reale, Giovanni. *The Systems of the Hellenistic Age*. Trans. John R Catan. New York: SUNY Press, 1985.

Rebellato, Dan. 'Globalization and Playwriting: Towards a Site-Unspecific Theatre.' *Contemporary Theatre Review* 16.1 (2006): 97–113.

———. 'From the State of the Nation to Globalization: Shifting Political Agendas in Contemporary British Playwriting.' *A Concise Companion to Contemporary British and Irish Drama*. Ed. Nadine Holdsworth and Mary Luckhurst. Oxford: Blackwell, 2007.

Reinelt, Janelle. 'Performing Europe: Identity Formation for a "New" Europe.' *Theatre Journal* 53.3 (2001): 365–87.

Ridout, Nicholas. *Theatre & Ethics*. Basingstoke, UK: Palgrave, 2009.

Robertson, Roland. *Globalization: Social Theory and Global Culture*. London: Sage, 1992.

Rosenbloom, David. *Aeschylus: The Persians*. London: Duckworth, 2006.

Russell, Susan. 'Corporate Theater: The Revolution of the Species.' MA Thesis. Florida State U, 2003.

Savarese, Nicola. *Paris/Artaud/Bali: Antonin Artaud vede il teatro balinese all'Esposizione Coloniale di Parigi del 1931*. Spettacolo. L'Aquila, Italy: Textus, 1997.

Schumpeter, Joseph A. *Capitalism, Socialism and Democracy*. London: Routledge, 1994.

Serra, Richard. *Writings/Interviews*. Chicago: U of Chicago P, 1994.

Shakespeare, William. *Hamlet*. Ed. G. R. Hibbard. Oxford: Oxford UP, 1987.

Shaw, George Bernard. *Major Barbara*. Ed. Margery Morgan. London: Penguin, 2000.

Singer, Peter. *One World: The Ethics of Globalization*. New Haven, CT, & London: Yale UP, 2002.

Soros, George. *The Crisis of Global Capitalism: Open Society Endangered*. London: Little, Brown, 1998.

Steger, Manfred B. *Globalization: A Very Short Introduction*. Oxford: Oxford UP, 2003.

Svich, Caridad, ed. *Trans-global Readings: Crossing Theatrical Boundaries*. Manchester: Manchester UP, 2003.

Talen, Bill. *What Should I Do If Reverend Billy Is in My Store?* New York: The New Press, 2003.

Törnqvist, Egil. *A Doll's House*. Cambridge: Cambridge UP, 1995.

Travers, Tony. *The Wyndham Report: The Economic Impact of London's West End Theatre*. London: Society of London Theatre, 1998.

Union of Concerned Scientists. 'Smoke, Mirrors & Hot Air: How ExxonMobil Uses Big Tobacco's Tactics to "Manufacture Uncertainty" on Climate Change.' Cambridge, MA: Union of Concerned Scientists, January 2007. 7 August 2008 <www.ucsusa.org/assets/documents/global_warming/exxon_report.pdf>.

Valaskakis, Kimon. 'Globalization as Theatre.' *International Social Science Journal* 160 (1999): 153–64.

Walton, John, and Charles Ragin. 'Global and National Sources of Political Protest: Third World Responses to the Debt Crisis.' *American Sociological Review* 55.6 (1990): 876–90.

Waters, Malcolm. *Globalization*. London: Routledge, 2001.

Wheen, Francis. *Karl Marx*. London: Fourth Estate, 1999.

Wickstrom, Maurya. *Performing Consumers: Global Capital and Its Theatrical Seductions*. Abingdon, UK: Routledge, 2006.

Wilde, Oscar. *The Complete Plays*. London: Methuen, 1988.

Wood, Allen W. *Kant*. Oxford: Blackwell, 2004.

World Bank. *From Plan to Market*. World Development Report 1996. New York: Oxford UP, 1996.

Worthen, William. 'Convicted Reading: *The Island*, Hybridity, Performance.' *Crucibles of Crisis: Performing Social Change*. Ed. Janelle Reinelt. Ann Arbor: U of Michigan P, 1996. 165–84.

# index

# acknowledgements

I would like to thank Chris Megson, Janelle Reinelt, and my wonderful editor, Jen Harvie, for their enormously helpful comments on earlier drafts of this book. The argument has benefited from many years of debate and discussion with Adam Mills. The UK Arts and Humanities Research Council and the Department of Drama and Theatre at Royal Holloway, University of London, funded the period of research on this project. Kate Haines at Palgrave is a model editor: patient, enthusiastic, and constructive.

This book is for Lilla.

# Theatre& small books on theatre & everything else

PUBLISHED IN 2009...

**theatre& the city**
Jen Harvie

**theatre politics**
Joe Kelleher

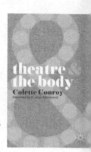

**theatre& human rights**
Paul Rae

**theatre the body**
Colette Conroy

978-0-230-20522-2

978-0-230-20523-9

978-0-230-20524-6

978-0-230-20543

> 'Short, sharp shots' for theatre students and enthusiasts
> Presenting the best writing from A-list scholars
> Vibrant and inspiring

**theatre& audience**
Helen Freshwater

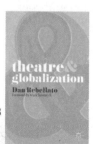

**theatre& globalization**
Dan Rebellato

**theatre& ethics**
Nicholas Ridout

**theatre& education**
Helen Nicholson

978-0-230-21028-8

978-0-230-21830-7

978-0-230-21027-1

978-0-230-21857-

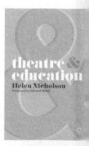

Place your order online at www.palgrave.com